LETTERS FOR LITIGATORS

Essential Communications for Opposing Counsel, Witnesses, Clients, and Others

DANIEL I. SMALL
ROBIN PAGE WEST

Cover design by ABA Publishing.

The materials contained herein represent the opinions of the authors and editors and should not be construed to be the action of either the American Bar Association or the General Practice, Solo and Small Firm Section unless adopted pursuant to the bylaws of the Association.

Nothing contained in this book is to be considered as the rendering of legal or financial advice for specific cases, and readers are responsible for obtaining such advice from their own legal or financial counsel. This book and any forms and agreements herein are intended for educational and informational purposes only

© 2004 American Bar Association. All rights reserved.
Printed in the United States of America.

08 07 06 05 04 5 4 3 2 1

Library of Congress Cataloging-in-Publication Data

Small, Daniel I., 1954-
Letters for litigators : essential communications for opposing counsel, witnesses, clients, and others / by Daniel I. Small and Robin Page West.
    p. cm.
  ISBN 1-59031-268-6 (pbk.)
    1. Law offices—United States—Records and correspondence—Forms.
2. Practice of law—United States—Records and correspondence—Forms. 3. Legal composition—Forms. I. West, Robin Page. II. Title.

KF170.S53 2004
808'.06634—dc22   2003018970

Discounts are available for books ordered in bulk. Special consideration is given to state bars, CLE programs, and other bar-related organizations. Inquire at ABA Publishing, Book Publishing, American Bar Association, 750 North Lake Shore Drive, Chicago, Illinois 60611.

www.ababooks.org

Contents

Acknowledgments ix

Introduction xi

About the Authors xv

CHAPTER 1
Outreach/Inquiry 1
    A. To the Client 2
        1. Inquiry – Personal Injury – Follow-up 2
        2. Inquiry – Follow-up 4
        3. Inquiry – Telephone Follow-up 5
        4. Inquiry – Referral Follow-up 6
        5. Inquiry Letter – Follow-up – Responsive Pleading 7
        6. Inquiry Letter – Investigation Marketing 8
        7. Inquiry – Medical Authorization 9

CHAPTER 2
Retention 11
    A. Retention Letters 12
        1. Retention Letter – Medical Defense 12
        2. Retention Letter – Insurance Company Confirm 13
        3. Retention Letter – Medical Plaintiff Follow-up 14
        4. Retention Letter – Insurance Client Confirm 16
        5. Retention Letter – Personal Injury Contingent Fee 17
        6. Retention Letter – Personal Injury Follow-up 19
        7. Retention Letter – Time Billing – No Retainer 24
        8. Retention Letter – Contingent Fee Cover Letter 27
        9. Retention Letter – Client Letter – Third-Party Payor 28
      10. Retention Letter – Time Billing – Retainer 30
      11. Retention Letter – Time Billing – Retainer – Evergreen 32
      12. Retention Letter – Time Billing – No Retainer 35
      13. Retention Letter – Contingency Fee – Local Counsel 37

	14. Retention Letter – Hourly/Retainer 39
	15. Retention Letter – Flat Fee Agreement Letter 41
	16. Retention Letter – Contingent Fee Agreement 43
	17. Retention Letter – Expert 45
	18. Retention Letter – Co-Counsel 46

B. Declination Letters 47
    1. Declination Letter – Contingent Fee – Employment 47
    2. Declination Letter – Contingent Fee – General 49
    3. Declination Letter – Contingent Fee – Whistleblower Specific 50
    4. Declination Letter – Contingent Fee – Whistleblower General 52
    5. Declination Letter – Contingent Fee – Medical Malpractice General 53
    6. Declination Letter – Contingent Fee – Medical Malpractice Specific 55
    7. Declination Letter – Contingent Fee – Negligence 57

C. Billing Letters 59
    1. Billing Letter – Cover Letter 59
    2. Billing Letter – Payment Plan 60
    3. Billing Letter – Collection 61
    4. Billing Letter – Evergreen 62
    5. Billing Letter – Request for Client to Advance Expenses 63

D. Withdrawing Representation 64
    1. Withdrawal – General 64
    2. Withdrawal – Contingency Fee 65

CHAPTER 3

Demand 67

A. Demands 68
    1. Demand Letter – Consumer Protection 68
    2. Demand Letter – Lease 70
    3. Demand Letter – Contract Nonpayment 72
    4. Demand Letter – Professional Fees 74
    5. Demand Letter – Business Defamation 76
    6. Demand Letter – Employment – Sexual Harassment 79
    7. Demand Letter – Personal Injury 86
    8. Demand Letter – Personal Injury – Alternate 94
    9. Demand Letter – Personal Injury – Post-Suit 98
    10. Demand Letter – Notice to Quit 100
    11. Demand Letter – Administrative Tribunal 101

B. Response 104
    1. Response – Employment 104

CHAPTER 4
Mediation/Arbitration 107
    A. To Opposing Counsel 108
        1. Mediation – Scheduling 108
    B. To the Client 109
        1. Mediation – Scheduling 109
        2. Mediation – Statement 110

CHAPTER 5
Complaint/Answer 111
    A. To the Court 112
        1. Court – Complaint 112
        2. Court – Sealed Complaint 113
        3. Court – Answer 114
    B. Opposing Counsel 115
        1. Opposing Counsel – Extension of Time 115
        2. Opposing Counsel – Complaint 116
    C. Client 117
        1. Client – Draft Complaint 117
        2. Client – Answer and Scheduling Letter 118
        3. Client – Forwarding Complaint – Insurer's Counsel 119

CHAPTER 6
Written Discovery Letters 121
    A. To Opposing Counsel – Requesting 122
        1. Discovery Letter – Discovery Requests 122
        2. Discovery Letter – Service on Counsel 123
        3. Discovery Letter – Overdue (Perfunctory) 124
        4. Discovery Letters – Overdue (Detailed) 125
        5. Discovery Letter – Incomplete 126
        6. Discovery Letter – Incomplete/Refused – General 128
        7. Discovery letter – Incomplete/Refused – Specific 129
        8. Discovery Letter – Follow-up to Document Request 132
        9. Discovery Letter – Follow-up to Interrogatory 133
      10. Discovery Letter – Supplement Request 134
      11. Discovery Letter – Follow-up 135
    B. To Opposing Counsel – Responding 136
        1. Discovery Letter – General Purpose 136
        2. Discovery Letter – Document Production 137
        3. Discovery Letter – Document Production Supplement 138
        4. Discovery Letter – Responses 139

CONTENTS

LETTERS FOR LITIGATORS

  5. Discovery Letter – Interrogatory Supplement 140
  6. Discovery Letter – Expert Witness Disclosure 143
  7. Discovery Letter – Follow-up – Continuance 145
 C. To Client 146
  1. Discovery Letter – Client – Request Interrogatory Response 146
  2. Discovery Letter – Client – Requesting Document Response 147
  3. Discovery Letter – Client – Forward Draft Interrogatory Response .. 148
  4. Discovery Letter – Client – Interrogatory Response 149
  5. Discovery Letter – Client – Discovery Meeting 151
  6. Discovery Letter – Client – Responses 152
  7. Discovery Letter – Client – Requesting Documents 153

CHAPTER 7
Deposition/Examination 155
 A. To Opposing Counsel 156
  1. Deposition Letter – Scheduling 156
  2. Deposition Letter – Scheduling (Alternate) 157
  3. Medical Examination – Scheduling 158
 B. To Client 159
  1. Deposition Letter – Notice 159
  2. Deposition Letter – Scheduling Letter 160
  3. Deposition Letter – Review Transcript 161
  4. Deposition Letter – Errata Sheet 162
  5. Deposition Letter – Status 163

CHAPTER 8
Motions 165
  1. Motions – Pretrial Submission 166
  2. Motions – Multiple Pleadings 167
  3. Motions – Court Order – To Client 168
  4. Motions – Requesting Action 169

CHAPTER 9
Trial 171
 A. Client 172
  1. Client – Scheduling 172
 B. Fact Witness 173
  1. Fact Witness – Inquiry 173

  C. Expert Witness 174
    1. Expert Witness – Client Letter 174
    2. Expert Witness – Deposition Review 175
    3. Expert Witness – Medical Examination 176
    4. Expert Witness – Scheduling 179

CHAPTER 10
Local Counsel 181
  A. Retention 182
    1. Local Counsel – Fee Agreement 182
  B. Follow-up 184
    1. Local Counsel Follow-up – Service 184
    2. Local Counsel Follow-up – Experts 185
    3. Local Counsel Follow-up – Discovery 186
    4. Local Counsel Follow-up – Deposition 187
    5. Local Counsel Follow-up – Status 188

CHAPTER 11
Settlement 189
  A. To the Client 190
    1. Settlement Letter – Demand 190
    2. Settlement Letter – Offer 191
    3. Settlement Letter – Begin Negotiations 192
    4. Settlement Letter – Finalize Distribution of Contingent Fees 193
    5. Settlement Letter – Closeout 194
  B. To Counsel 195
    1. Settlement Letter – Memorializing Settlement – Error in Release 195
    2. Settlement Letter – Enclosing Executed Release 196

CHAPTER 12
Ethical 197
    1. Ethical Letters – Challenge to Conflict 198
    2. Ethical Letters – Conflict – Individual 200
    3. Ethical Letters – Contact with Employees 202

CHAPTER 13
Administrative/Other Proceedings 205
    1. Opposing Request for Postponement 206
    2. Enclosing Brief 208

CHAPTER 14
Government Investigations 209
    A. To Client 210
        1. To Client – Confirming Letter 210
        2. To Client – Joint Defense Cover Letter 212
        3. To Client – Scheduling Letter 213
        4. To Client – Forwarding Transcripts 214
    B. To Others 215
        1. To Others – Letter to Agency 215
        2. To Others – Third-Party Documents 216
        3. To Others – Government Records Response 217

Note: *Page numbers correspond to filenames for each letter on CD-ROM*

Acknowledgments

We would like to thank attorneys Victor Koufman, Robert Wolkon, Marc Ganz, Richard J. Magid, and Sandon L. Cohen for providing invaluable input and materials, and our assistants, Kristen Peters and Catherine Pitchford, for countless hours spent on the thankless task of bringing organization out of chaos. Dan Small thanks his wife, Alix, and children Bailey, Gabrielle, and Schuyler, and Robin Page West thanks her husband, Jim, and children Garrett and Esmé, for having the love and patience to let the authors pursue their love of writing while practicing law.

Introduction

Letters and pleadings give structure and flow to a litigator's practice. Just as we pursue our clients' goals through the effective and judicious use of pleadings and motions, so too can we use letters to define and pursue our goals; to communicate those goals to our opposing counsel, clients, and staff; and to measure whether we are attaining them in a timely fashion.

Letter documentation of actions taken and requests made serves myriad valuable functions. A letter not only makes a request, it also memorializes when and to whom the request was made. It can also include the circumstances of the request, such as, "This is my fourth request in as many months for these documents." When copied to those other than the recipient, the letter serves the purpose of passing this information along, and when later attached to a motion, it provides support for the court.

With a file properly documented, neither the lawyer nor the administrative and paralegal staff need rely on each others' memories, or presence in the office, to divine what happened, and what should happen, by when.

The volume of communications taking place over the phone and via e-mail leaves little time to draft succinctly worded letters. Often we regard letter writing as an impossible luxury. As nice as it would be to document the file, confirm with opposing counsel, and apprise the client of your two phone conversations and four e-mails this morning, there isn't time to put it down on paper before you leave for court this afternoon. Do you keep the information in your head and try to remember to do a letter later? Do you reluctantly forward the e-mails to the client but wonder whether the casual tone and the pleasantries you are sharing with adverse counsel might seem a tad glib to the client?

As electronic communication via quick e-mails and voice mail becomes the norm, and paper letters the exception, it becomes increasingly important not to lose sight of the importance of documenting the file and maintaining a professional tone. The letters in this book can simplify and expedite this effort, whether sent in paper form or via e-mail. Rather than drafting the letters from scratch yourself, or asking your staff to, use these letters instead as a foundation to save time and simplify your office routine.

Letter-Writing Strategy

In litigation, there is no such thing as a "casual letter." Every letter that goes out becomes a part of the litigation and should be done with care and with strategic considerations in mind. These may include the following:

LETTERS FOR LITIGATORS

- *When in doubt, write it out.* A little effort now to put things in writing can save a lot of time, money, and hostility later, when memories or positions change. Run your practice by the words of the great poet Robert Frost (from his wonderful poem, "Mending Wall"): "Good fences make good neighbors." In litigation, words are our "fences," and are how we define and record our actions, positions, and more.

- *Be clear.* Whatever the subject, from a court transmittal letter to a client retention letter to a letter memorializing a telephone conversation, make sure you are clear about what you're saying, what you're agreeing to, or what you're requesting. There may be times when there are reasons to be intentionally vague, but generally a vague letter can be worse than no letter at all, because the recipient (or those copied) can take it to mean something different than you intended.

- *Be relentlessly polite.* Whether dealing with an anonymous clerk or an obnoxious opposing counsel, a little politeness can go a long way. With the clerk, there is no reason to not be nice, and who knows, that extra "thank you" just might speed the help you need. With opposing counsel, you can never take back a nasty letter: it will continue to look unprofessionally snide and snippy long after the immediate reasons for your outrage have faded away.

- *Leave the ball in their court.* A good letter clearly states the sender's position, and then shifts the burden to the recipient to take the next step. This process can include a transmittal letter requesting a response, or a positioning letter closing with words like: "If I have in any way misunderstood or misstated our agreement/our conversation/the facts, please let me know as soon as possible." In each instance, the other side is put in the position of needing to do something.

- *Don't overstate.* Sometimes it is tempting to let our imaginations, our frustrations, or our rhetoric run wild in a letter. Some clients like to see this kind of "strength" in their lawyer. But if the law and facts do not back up our rhetoric, it is a false and potentially harmful "strength." An overstated letter can lose credibility and can be held up over and over as evidence that the court—or other key players—cannot trust the writer.

At some point, overstatement may also be an ethical—and even legal—problem. Statutes such as the federal Fair Debt Collection Practices Act govern sending letters attempting to collect a debt, and lawyers' letters may be subject to these restrictions. Make sure you do not run afoul of them. Moreover, be mindful of the risks involved in making allegations outside the context of litigation. Although allegedly defamatory statements made in the context of litigation may be protected by privilege, as may statements you make to your client, accusations you make against the opposing party before suit is filed are not protected. Pre-suit letters threatening litigation may not be protected, especially when the sender is not seriously considering judicial proceedings in good faith. For example, in *Meltzer, et al. v. Grant, et al.*, 2002 U.S. Dist.

LEXIS 5514, a U.S. magistrate judge refused to dismiss a claim for intentional infliction of emotional distress against a lawyer who wrote a pre-suit demand letter. Check your locality's rules, guidelines, and cases for guidance with respect to demand letters, in particular.

How to Use this Book
No book of forms can serve as a substitute for factual or legal research or knowledge. Before using any of these letters, the attorney must research the applicable law, including court rules, statutes of limitations, and other state- and case-specific information, and substitute the applicable information for the client's case into the form letter. For example, letters in this book recite statute of limitations deadlines that may or may not be applicable to your particular case or state. Be sure to research and include the proper information, which may be different from the information in the form letters.

A final tip: make sure each letter you send out is diaried internally for follow-up. Did you ask the client to provide documents within a week? Did you send a letter that requested a response within 15 days? These letters should be "calendared" or "diaried" for follow-up so if the documents didn't arrive, you can follow up, and if the answer wasn't filed, you can move for default. Make it a point to check your diaried letters on a daily or weekly basis, and you'll find that those things that used to fall through the cracks no longer do.

Robin Page West
rpw@cohanwest.com
Cohan & West, P. C.
201 N. Charles Street, Suite 2404
Baltimore, MD 21201
(410) 332-1400 (v)
(410) 332-4079 (fax)
http://www.cohanwest.com
http://www.QuiTamOnline.com

Daniel I. Small
dsmall@broadandcassel.com
Broad and Cassel
Miami Center, Suite 3000
201 South Biscayne Blvd.
Miami, FL 33131
(305) 373-9454 (voice)
(305) 995-6431 (fax)

About the Authors

Dan Small is a trial lawyer and partner in the Miami, Florida, office of Broad and Cassel. His practice focuses on SEC and other government agency investigations, complex civil litigation, and white-collar criminal matters. A former federal prosecutor, he was a lecturer on law at Harvard Law School, where he taught federal litigation. He has taught trial advocacy at Harvard and at other law schools and CLE programs. He is a frequent newspaper, television, and Internet commentator.

Mr. Small has been involved in several high-profile cases around the country, serving as lead defense attorney for former Louisiana Governor Edwin Edwards, leader of the "dream team" in the "Jerry Springer murder" case (*Sarasota Herald*), counsel in a prominent SEC Internet fraud case, special counsel to the Rhode Island Ethics Commission, and special counsel to the Massachusetts House Ethics Committee. He was vice-chair of the ABA's White Collar Crime Committee.

Mr. Small is author of two best-selling American Bar Association books—*Preparing Witnesses* and *Going to Trial*—that have become the foundation of successful ABA, state, and law firm CLE programs around the country. He can be reached by e-mail at dsmall@broadandcassel.com or by phone at (305) 373-9454.

Robin Page West is a trial lawyer with the Baltimore, Maryland, law firm of Cohan & West, P.C. Her practice focuses on complex commercial and personal injury civil litigation and cases brought under the federal Civil False Claims Act. She was on the faculty of the Alabama Bar Institute's False Claims Act Seminar and the American Bar Association's Health Care Fraud and Qui Tam National Institutes for lawyers.

Ms. West has been involved in several cases of national significance, serving as lead counsel for the whistleblower in the case of *U.S. ex rel. Fletcher v. MetPath*, the fourth largest qui tam recovery nationwide in 1995. She has also represented the plaintiffs/relators in numerous other cases alleging that false statements were made to the government that resulted in a $6.8 million settlement with Quest Diagnostics, Inc., an $8.9 million settlement with Cigna Corp., and a $2 million settlement with Genesis Health Ventures, Inc., among others.

Ms. West is also the author of the American Bar Association's book *Advising the Qui Tam Whistleblower: From Identifying a Case to Filing Under the False Claims Act*. She can be reached by e-mail at rpw@cohanwest.com, or by phone at (410) 332-1400.

CHAPTER 1

Outreach/Inquiry

After you meet with or speak to a prospective client, it's a good idea to send a follow-up letter to clarify your role and to explain what the client needs to do if he or she wants to retain you. If the statute of limitations or some other circumstance creates a time issue, tell the client in writing. Potential clients may have consulted with several lawyers and may not have a clear memory of what each lawyer told them. By memorializing your consultation in writing, not only do you document the file, but you also create an additional opportunity to secure the client's business.

On the other hand, if you do not want to represent the client, or cannot, a follow-up letter documents this as well, so there will be no confusion later about whether you did or did not undertake the representation.

CHAPTER 1

LETTERS FOR LITIGATORS

A. To the Client

1. Inquiry – Personal Injury – Follow-up

Date

Name
Company Name
Address 1
Address 2
City, State, Zip Code

Re:

Dear _____:

This is in follow-up to your communications with our office regarding a motor vehicle accident in which your daughter and son were involved on [Date].

Our file shows that the children were examined by [Doctor's Name] on [Date]. The doctor asked they be brought back in if they did not get better over the following two weeks. We have not heard from you since then and are writing to find out whether you have resolved this matter or whether you wish to pursue it further.

If you are interested in retaining us, please provide 1) a copy of the police report, 2) a written statement summarizing the accident, 3) details regarding where, when, and from whom medical treatment was obtained, 4) copies of all bills or a listing of the cost of the treatment, and 5) an itemization of any other losses or expenses incurred. If we determine that we are willing to undertake this case, we will provide you with a written fee agreement to review and sign. Unless and until the written agreement is signed, no attorney-client relationship exists for this accident, and we are therefore at this time taking no action on behalf of you or your children.

Please be mindful that the law imposes time limits for filing suits, and therefore, if you intend to pursue this matter, you should not delay in obtaining counsel. If we do not hear from you within the next 30 days, we will assume that you do not wish us to take any further action and we will close our file.

Outreach/Inquiry

Sincerely,

Law Firm

Lawyer Name

2. Inquiry – Follow-up

Date

Name
Company Name
Address 1
Address 2
City, State, Zip Code

    Re:

Dear _____:

This is in follow-up to [Referring Attorney]'s letter to you of [Date] in which he gave you my name. I have not heard from you, and am writing this letter to make sure there is no misunderstanding about my role.

Please be advised that unless and until we enter into a signed, written fee agreement, I am not your attorney, and we have no attorney-client relationship.

Should you wish for me to evaluate your case to see if I can represent you, please provide me with copies of all documents relating to the fees you paid [Defendant], including the amounts and the dates, as well as copies of any documents, letters, or memos he gave you, and let me know the total amounts you paid him and when.

If you do not provide me with these documents and information, I will assume that you do not wish for me to get involved in this. Since I do not know when all of the relevant events happened, I need to point out to you that the statute of limitations on any case against [Defendant] could be about to expire very soon, if it has not already, and for that reason, you should not delay in making your decision on what to do.

                              Sincerely,

                              Law Firm

                              Lawyer Name

3. Inquiry – Telephone Follow-up

CHAPTER 1
Outreach/Inquiry

Date

**CERTIFIED MAIL AND
RETURN RECEIPT REQUESTED**

Name
Company Name
Address 1
Address 2
City, State, Zip Code

    Re:

Dear _____:

This is in follow-up to our telephone discussion of [Date]. Since I have not heard further from you, and we have not entered into a fee agreement, no attorney-client relationship has formed, and I am closing my file on this matter.

I have not been provided with sufficient information to determine whether you have a cause of action for [type of claim], and I am not by this letter expressing any advice or opinion in that regard.

Because the law imposes certain time limits on when claims may be filed, your legal right to file a claim may expire with the passage of time. Accordingly, if you have any intentions of filing a claim or lawsuit regarding this matter, you should contact the attorney of your choice at once; otherwise, your claim or suit may be barred.

    Sincerely,

    Law Firm

    Lawyer Name

CHAPTER 1
LETTERS FOR LITIGATORS

4. Inquiry – Referral Follow-up

Date

Name
Company Name
Address 1
Address 2
City, State, Zip Code

Re:

Dear _____:

It was a pleasure speaking with you this morning about your potential claim against a child support enforcement agency in Florida.

As we discussed, this case might be a qui tam case or a class action suit. As I indicated on the phone, I see some potential problems with bringing the case as a qui tam, and although I am not expressing an opinion one way or the other about whether you have a case or not, I suggested you contact a Florida lawyer familiar with both state class actions and federal qui tam procedure to assist you in evaluating this matter. I gave you the names of three such lawyers, and they are:

1. [name and address]
2. [name and address]
3. [name and address]

Please be aware that the law imposes certain limits on the time in which you must file suit. If you miss these deadlines, you will lose your right to sue. From the information you gave me, I am unable to determine when these deadlines expire. Therefore, you should contact another lawyer of your choosing as soon as possible so your right to make a claim is not lost with the passage of time.

Sincerely,

Law Firm

Lawyer Name

5. Inquiry Letter – Follow-up – Responsive Pleading

Date

Name
Company Name
Address 1
Address 2
City, State, Zip Code

Re:

Dear _____:

I am writing to follow up on our telephone conversation today. When we spoke, you advised me that your situation at [employer] appeared to be improving since our initial consultation in my office, and that you have decided not to pursue any claims against your employer for alleged discrimination.

I am writing to remind you, as we have previously discussed, that in the event you do elect to pursue an action for discrimination, any potential claims you may have against your current employer for age discrimination or other types of unlawful discrimination must be brought within six (6) months of the last discriminatory act, or your claims may be forfeited. The law is very strict with regard to this time limitation. Therefore, if you believe that there has been an unlawful act that was based, in whole or in part, on age discrimination, you will be required to bring a claim against your employer within six months of this action. While I hope that things continue to improve for you at work, I just want to make sure you remain aware of this very important time limitation.

Based on our recent discussions, I assume that you are not retaining me to represent you in this matter. If this is not the case, please contact me immediately.

Sincerely,

Law Firm

Lawyer Name

6. Inquiry Letter – Investigation Marketing

Date

Name
Company Name
Address 1
Address 2
City, State, Zip Code

Re:

Dear _____:

I am writing in regard to the current _____ investigation relating to _____. As the attached indicates, we have developed substantial experience and expertise in representing witnesses in _____ and other financial investigations and litigation. Please let me know if we can be of assistance in your matter.

Thank you.

                        Sincerely,

                        Law Firm

                        Lawyer Name

Enclosure

7. Inquiry – Medical Authorization

Outreach/Inquiry

Date

Name
Company Name
Address 1
Address 2
City, State, Zip Code

Re:

Dear _____:

Enclosed are authorization forms allowing me to obtain your medical records, bills and information to determine whether the medical problems you are having were caused by the [fill in cause of action].

Please sign them, write your date of birth where indicated, have your signature witnessed, and mail the signed forms back to me in the envelope provided.

As always, please do not hesitate to call if you have any questions.

Sincerely,

Law Firm

Lawyer Name

CHAPTER 2

Retention

Sometimes the lawyer is assigned to defend a case by the insurance company and simply announces this fact in a letter to the insured. Other times, the retention letter memorializes how much the lawyer is paid, and when, as well as the lawyer and client's obligations to each other. Declination letters, on the other hand, memorialize the fact that the lawyer is *not* representing the client.

As the examples show, retention letters vary, and fees may be structured in myriad ways. Nevertheless, putting the fact of the retention, and its terms, in writing is vital to avoid ambiguity and misunderstanding. Most jurisdictions, if not all, require contingent fee agreements to be in writing, and many statutes impose caps and/or requirements of "reasonableness" on the amount of fees. Use these letters as a starting point in creating your own retention letters, taking care to research your jurisdiction's particular requirements and prohibitions regarding attorneys' fees.

If there is to be no representation, it is equally important to communicate that to the client along with the need to retain other counsel in a timely manner. The signed "return receipt requested card" evidencing the client's receipt of a declination (non-retention) letter can be useful should a client who never retained you comes back later complaining that you failed to protect his interests.

A. Retention Letters

1. Retention Letter – Medical Defense

Date

Name
Company Name
Address 1
Address 2
City, State, Zip Code

Re:

Dear Dr. X:

The firm of [Firm Name] has been retained by [Insurance Company] on your behalf with regard to the Notice of Intent to Initiate Litigation for Medical Malpractice for the above-mentioned patient. Please do not discuss this matter with anyone other than a representative of [Firm Name]. [Lawyer Name], Esquire will also be working on this file with me.

Prior to initiating a lawsuit against you, the Plaintiff is required to send a Notice of Intent to Initiate Litigation. In response, it is your obligation to review the matter and either (1) deny the claim, indicating that there is no demonstration of any medical negligence; (2) make a settlement offer; or (3) offer to arbitrate solely on the issues of how much damage was caused to the Plaintiff and/or potential claimants. Our response to the Notice of Intent in one of the above-mentioned forms must be provided within 90 days of your receipt of the Notice of Intent. At this time, we estimate the expiration of the 90-day period to be no later than [Date].

Please contact my assistant, [Name of Assistant], to arrange a conference with me to review this matter. Also, please forward a copy of your curriculum vitae.

Sincerely,

Law Firm

Lawyer Name

cc: Insurance Company

2. Retention Letter – Insurance Company Confirm

Date

Name
Company Name
Address 1
Address 2
City, State, Zip Code

   Re:

Dear _____:

Thank you for your letter of December 30, 2001, and for the assignment of the above-referenced matter to [Firm Name]. The following medical malpractice defense team members will be working on this case: [Partner Name, Esq.; Associate Name; Paralegal Name]. Our customary rates will apply to this matter.

We have developed an excellent relationship with [Hospital Representative] at [Hospital Name] regarding another matter, and we appreciate the opportunity to work with her again. Our firm has commenced work on this case: Attorney [Name] has been in contact with [Hospital Administrator Name or Attorney Name (co-defense or plaintiff's counsel)] and I will file a notice of appearance on behalf of [Hospital Name] within the next couple of days. Please feel free to call [Associate Attorney Name] or me if you have any questions or concerns.

Thank you for the opportunity to be of service to [Insurance Company Client Name].

                            Sincerely,

                            Law Firm

                            Lawyer Name

CHAPTER 2

LETTERS FOR LITIGATORS

3. Retention Letter – Medical Plaintiff Follow-up

Date

Name
Company Name
Address 1
Address 2
City, State, Zip Code

Re:

Dear _____:

Thank you for taking the time to meet with us yesterday to discuss the progress on your case. At the outset, I must say I thought the meeting was very productive for all of us. I would like to take this opportunity to go over some of the issues that we discussed and the decisions we made.

First: you have authorized us to engage the services of outside counsel to assist in this matter. As we discussed yesterday, there will be no direct cost to you for these services. It is our intention to enter into a written agreement wherein outside counsel will receive a portion of the attorneys' fees due to this firm in the event that we prevail on the case. Additionally, it is my intention to seek contribution from outside counsel for ongoing expenses in an amount proportionate to our fee agreement with them.

You also authorized us to retain the services of a second expert. As you know, this expert has requested a [$____] retainer, and it is my intention to engage his services in the very near future.

We also discussed a budget for expenses in this case. At the present time, my thinking is that expenses could very well be in the range of [Amount] if we have to complete formal discovery and prepare for trial. You were kind enough to agree to pay [__%] of all of the expenses *as* those expenses are incurred.

Finally, following a discussion of the pros and cons of mediation and arbitration, you have authorized us to attempt to arrange non-binding mediation with [Defendant Name]. As we discussed, I anticipate that our share of the expense for the mediator would be [$____ to $____]. I will attempt to make the arrangements as soon as possible.

I hope that this letter accurately reflects the decisions we made yesterday. If not, I would be most appreciative if you could let me know at your earliest convenience.

CHAPTER 2
Retention

Sincerely,

Law Firm

Lawyer Name

CHAPTER 2

LETTERS FOR LITIGATORS

4. Retention Letter – Insurance Client Confirm

Date

Name
Company Name
Address 1
Address 2
City, State, Zip Code

Re:

Dear _____:

[Firm Name] has been appointed to represent you in the above matter by [Insurance Company Name]. To learn more about our firm and attorneys, please visit our Web site at [URL].

Your hearing date is scheduled for [Date/Time/Court]. Prior to the hearing, it is important that we meet with you, at your convenience, to discuss [Plaintiff's] allegations, and to investigate the events surrounding his claims in detail, in order to prepare your defense. [Attorney Name] would like to meet with you as soon as possible. Please call our office upon receipt of this letter to arrange for a time and place to meet with [Attorney Name].

Thank you for your cooperation. We look forward to working with you.

Sincerely,

Law Firm

Lawyer Name

cc: Client Insurance Company Claim Rep.

5. Retention Letter – Personal Injury Contingent Fee

CONTINGENT FEE AGREEMENT

Client: [Name] retains the law office of [Firm Name and Address] to perform the legal services set forth in Paragraph 1 below. The firm agrees to perform them faithfully and with due diligence.

1. The claim, controversy and other matters with reference to which the services are to be performed are personal injuries sustained as a result of [an automobile accident] that occurred on or about [Date].

2. The contingency upon which fees are to be paid is any recovery of money.

3. The client shall not pay fees except from amounts collected for him/her by the firm except in accordance with Paragraph 5.

4. The client shall pay reasonable compensation on the foregoing contingency services to the firm, in the amount of [33-1/3%] of the gross amount received inclusive of multiple damages and/or attorney's fees; in addition thereto, the client will pay all expenses and disbursements.

5. The client is, in any event, to be liable to the firm for its reasonable expenses and disbursements incurred in connection with this matter, including, but not limited to, long-distance telephone charges, travel, copying charges, fees for obtaining medical records, court filing fees, costs of service of process and other papers, and costs of depositions or other discovery.

6. The client agrees that the firm may withdraw its representation of the client and terminate this Agreement should the firm determine within [one hundred twenty (120) days] of the date of this Agreement that there is no reasonable likelihood of recovery on behalf of the client.

7. If the firm is discharged by the client prior to the conclusion of this representation, the firm is entitled to then be compensated for its reasonable expenses and disbursements and for the fair value of the services rendered to the client up to the time of discharge, but the amount of the fee shall not be due to the attorney until the subject claim or litigation is concluded pursuant to Paragraphs 2 and 3 above.

LETTERS FOR LITIGATORS

8. The client warrants and represents that he/she is not liable to any other attorney/firm for expenses, disbursements, or services performed in connection with this matter.

This Agreement and its performance are subject to Rule 3:05 of the Supreme Judicial Court of Massachusetts.

I HAVE READ AND UNDERSTOOD THIS AGREEMENT BEFORE SIGNING IT AND MY QUESTIONS REGARDING THIS AGREEMENT HAVE BEEN ASKED BY ME AND ANSWERED TO MY SATISFACTION.

_____   _____
FIRM NAME   **CLIENT NAME**

I acknowledge receipt of a signed copy of this Agreement this ____ day of [Month, Year].

_____
Attorney

6. Retention Letter – Personal Injury Follow-up

Date

Name
Company Name
Address 1
Address 2
City, State, Zip Code

    Re:

Dear _____:

Thank you for allowing us to represent you in the referenced matter. Since you probably do not know what to expect as we process your claim for injuries, we would like to acquaint you with the general pattern of how we handle cases of this type. We feel it is helpful to both our clients and ourselves if they know in advance what to expect.

Questions

When you were interviewed the first time, we obtained general information from you regarding the date of the accident, the place of the accident, and the general nature of the injuries. This information is used in connection with the investigation as described later.

Obtaining Information

We will notify the other party's insurance company that you have retained us as your attorneys. We will also request that the insurance company give us a copy of any statements you may have given them.

We will send letters to all physicians and hospitals involved in the case, notifying them that you have retained us to represent you. We will request from them copies of all records, reports and bills. If you have lost time from your employment, we will obtain such verification from your employer, and we will then send all of these documents to the insurance company representing the party responsible for the accident and your injuries.

If there was a police investigation, we will obtain a copy of the police report and, if we feel it is required, take photographs of the vehicles and scene, interview witnesses, and obtain all the facts necessary in the han-

CHAPTER 2

LETTERS FOR LITIGATORS

dling of your case. If necessary, we may even hire a private investigator to assist us in this investigation.

Evaluation

It is important to know that no case is settled until the exact nature of the client's medical condition has been determined. It may take several weeks or months to gather all information necessary, and in some cases it is impossible to obtain the necessary information because the doctor cannot answer many questions until treatment has been completed. Sometimes we have to wait one to two years from the date of the accident before we can receive a final medical condition statement. One of the most difficult requests we make of our clients is patience.

As soon as the investigation has been completed and all necessary medical information obtained, we will evaluate your case. We will attempt to arrive at a proper settlement figure. No settlement figure is ever accepted without the client's consent.

Starting a Lawsuit

If settlement cannot be reached with the insurance company, we will consider the advisability of filing a lawsuit. In some cases, however, it is important to start a lawsuit immediately.

A lawsuit is started by filing with the court and delivering to the other party a paper called a Complaint that indicates that he/she is being sued as a result of the accident. The other party is called a defendant. The defendant takes these papers to his insurance company, which delivers them to its lawyers. The lawyers then file with the court and deliver to us a paper called an Answer, and at that point, the case is at issue.

We want to point out that although a lawsuit may be started, settlement is always possible and very often made just before trial. Ninety percent of the cases are settled without the necessity of trial.

Discovery

Once the lawsuit has been started, both sides have the right to obtain information or "discovery" about the case by deposition, document requests, interrogatories or medical examination.

A <u>discovery deposition</u> is the testimony of some party or witness given under oath in the presence of attorneys for both plaintiff and defendant and before a court reporter, who takes down the testimony in writing.

<u>Interrogatories</u> are written questions that either party's attorney may submit, and which have to be answered in writing under oath by the other party.

We generally use both interrogatories and depositions to help us investigate the facts. The defendant's attorney also has the right to take testimony and submit interrogatories, and if so, we will need your assistance and will be in contact with you.

<u>Medical Examination</u>: The defendant has the right to have you examined by a physician of his/her choice. The insurance company will pay the cost of this examination, and a report will be given to the insurance company with the doctor's findings and his/her opinions concerning your injuries. We also will receive a copy of that physician's report.

Under the rules of the court, there are no longer any secrets in lawsuits. The attorneys for both sides take depositions and submit interrogatories to assist them in finding out all facts. At any time throughout this period, the possibility of settlement may come up again, and we will endeavor to discuss settlement as we move along. If anything concrete occurs in any of these discussions, we will advise you promptly.

Trial

The great majority of cases are never tried, even though lawsuits are started. Often, however, they are not settled until just before the trial date. If your case cannot be settled for a fair amount of money that is acceptable to you, we will, with your permission, proceed to trial. Before we go to trial, the few weeks before the trial date are spent in detailed preparation of your case. We will explain what is expected of you at trial in minute detail well in advance of your going to the courthouse.

It is absolutely essential that we have your complete cooperation in helping us gather facts about your case.

<u>The insurance company has an index system on a nationwide basis that shows all of the people who have made claims before for other injuries</u>. If you have made a claim in another accident for another injury, your name will be there, and they will have this information. You are therefore urged to be absolutely honest with us in all of your answers throughout our handling of your case.

CHAPTER 2

Retention

Conclusion

The information contained in this brief letter is necessarily general in its terms. Each and every case we have in our office is handled on an individual basis. Although one attorney is assigned to your case and has the responsibility for it, you have the benefit and assistance of the entire firm in connection with your case.

We will make an effort to keep you informed periodically and will send you copies of all pleadings and correspondence; however, it is impossible for us to call you and give you a report on your case every week. On the other hand, if you have any questions at any time about your case, do not hesitate to call the attorney who is handling your file. We would like you to read carefully the following suggestions:

1. Do not discuss your case with anyone other than your attorney, your doctors or your own insurance company.

2. Do not sign <u>anything</u> with respect to your claim until you have checked with the attorney handling your file.

3. Send to us <u>all</u> receipts and bills incurred as a result of your injuries. Also, send to us <u>any</u> correspondence you receive from <u>any source</u> concerning your case.

4. Notify us at once of any change of address or employment, or of any other fact that might affect your case.

5. If, after consulting us, you miss any work because of your injuries, notify us right away.

6. If you have to go to the hospital after consulting us, or if your present physician refers you to another physician, notify us right away.

7. If you are self-employed, keep a record of the time you are unable to work or perform your duties.

8. If there is a claim for loss of income, the defendant's attorney has a right to see what amount you have earned. Consequently, arrange to have available for copies your income tax returns (or W-2 forms) for the three-year period before the accident.

We will do all we can to bring your case to a satisfactory conclusion, and again, thank you for consulting us.

Sincerely,

Law Firm

Lawyer Name

CHAPTER 2
LETTERS FOR LITIGATORS

7. Retention Letter – Time Billing – No Retainer

Date

Name
Company Name
Address 1
Address 2
City, State, Zip Code

Re:

Dear _____:

Kindly notify me if you have any questions with respect to the following fee agreement. Should you not have any questions, please sign it and return it to me in the enclosed self-addressed envelope. This is our standard fee agreement **except that in your case, I am not asking for a retainer.** Also, kindly complete the enclosed questionnaire, which I will use to draft a separation agreement. I look forward to working with you.

Fee Agreement

Hourly Rate: The client [Client Name] will be billed for services rendered at the firm's hourly rate in effect at the time the work is performed. In the event of a change of more than 10 percent of the initial rate billed to the client, the client may terminate this Agreement, upon payment in full of all disbursements incurred and all fees earned. The hourly rates presently in effect are Principal at [$____], Associate at [$____], and Paralegal at [$____]. Our time is billed in increments of no less than six (6) minutes.

Services Rendered: All services performed in connection with a matter are billed as part of that matter, including phone calls and reviews of correspondence.

Disbursements: All disbursements incurred in connection with this matter are billed directly to you. Such out-of-pocket disbursements are in addition to any amounts owed to us for our fee.

Professional Statements for Services Rendered: On the first day of each month, we will send a statement that indicates our fee for services rendered during the previous month, as well as all out-of-pocket disbursements incurred. All amounts reflected on the statement are due and payable upon receipt by you. We reserve the right without further notice to charge interest on any outstanding balances past due [___ days] at [__%] per annum, and/or to terminate all future services to be rendered in connection with your matter. You may terminate this Agreement at any time, whereupon you must pay in full all disbursements incurred and all fees earned, whether accrued or outstanding. We reserve the right to send interim bills to you at any time the outstanding balance on your statement for services rendered equals or exceeds $1,500.00. We further reserve all rights regarding the failure to pay same as we do on our regular monthly statements.

Client Files: It is the policy of this office to retain files for a period of seven (7) years from the date that your matter is resolved. Six months after your matter is resolved, your records will be placed in a storage facility and there will be a charge (from the storage facility) to retrieve your records should the need arise.

If after reading this letter you still wish to retain the services of our firm in connection with your matter, please indicate below that you have received this statement, you have read and understood it, and that you agree with all its terms and conditions by signing your name in full on the line provided below and dating same in the space provided. Please make all checks payable to [Firm Name].

Please understand that unless this Agreement is signed and received by the firm, no work can be done in connection with your matter.

                        Sincerely,

                        Law Firm

                        Lawyer Name

Enclosures

I acknowledge receipt of, have read and understand the above letter, and agree to its terms and conditions set forth above.

_____
SIGNATURE

_____
CLIENT

Address _____

City/Town, State and Zip _____

Tel. No. (Home) _____

Dated:_____

8. Retention Letter – Contingent Fee Cover Letter

Date

Name
Company Name
Address 1
Address 2
City, State, Zip Code

Re:

Dear _____:

Pursuant to our telephone conversation today, enclosed please find duplicate originals of a Contingent Fee Agreement for you to sign. The rules governing attorneys in Massachusetts require these Agreements before I may begin working on your claims. Please sign both Agreements and have your signatures witnessed. Please then return the white copies to me.

I have also enclosed five copies of a Medical Authorization Release Form. This will enable me to obtain medical reports and bills from your doctors and other medical providers, which I will need to pursue your claims. Please sign all five of these forms as well and return them to my attention.

Thank you for asking me to represent you in this matter. I look forward to working with you. If you have any questions, please do not hesitate to give me a call.

Sincerely,

Law Firm

Lawyer Name

Enclosures

9. Retention Letter – Client Letter – Third-Party Payor

Date

Name
Company Name
Address 1
Address 2
City, State, Zip Code

Re:

Dear _____:

Thank you for asking this Law Firm to represent you in connection with the above matter. I am writing regarding the terms and conditions of this Law Firm's representation of you, including our fees and the services to be provided.

This firm will provide legal representation to you at the rate of [$_____] per hour for all work performed by me or other attorneys in the firm, including but not limited to legal research, preparation of court or agency papers, correspondence or other documents, conferences, telephone calls, attendance at meetings or court/agency proceedings, and travel time. In addition, the firm will bill you for reimbursement of all significant out-of-pocket expenses incurred in connection with this matter, including but not limited to filing fees, outside research fees, subpoena costs and transcripts. We do not bill our clients for incidental expenses such as routine photocopying of documents, telephone toll calls, telefaxing, and postage.

You have advised me that there will be a third party who should be billed for our services. We will send itemized monthly statements to that party per the above arrangement, detailing all charges for hourly fees and expenses, which are due and payable within thirty days. However, we have agreed that you are ultimately responsible for payment of all fees in the event our invoices are not paid by the third party.

If the terms of this letter are agreeable to you, please sign below to indicate that you have read and understand this letter and that you agree to its terms. Please return the original signed and dated representation letter to me.

We look forward to working with you on this matter. If you have any questions, please do not hesitate to contact me.

                Sincerely,

                Law Firm

                Lawyer Name

AGREED TO:

_____

Dated:_____

10. Retention Letter – Time Billing – Retainer

Date

Name
Company Name
Address 1
Address 2
City, State, Zip Code

Re:

Dear _____:

Thank you for asking this firm to represent [Company Name] in connection with your corporate business and litigation matters. I am writing to set forth our agreement regarding the terms and conditions of this Law Firm's representation of [Company Name], including our fees and services to be provided.

This firm will represent [Company Name] at the rate of $_____ per hour for all work performed by me or any other attorney in the firm, including legal research, preparation of correspondence, pleadings and/or corporate papers, conferences, telephone calls, attendance at meetings, depositions, hearings, trials and travel time. In addition, the firm will bill you for reimbursement of all significant out-of-pocket expenses incurred in connection with these matters, including filing fees, overnight mail and hand-delivery fees. We will assume all costs for incidental expenses such as routine photocopying of documents, telephone toll calls, telefaxing, and postage.

You have agreed to provide us with a retainer in the amount of $_____. I will request an additional retainer in the event this amount is depleted below $_____. We will place these funds in our clients' fund account, and will bill you for services rendered on a monthly basis in the amount of that month's hourly fees plus expenses. You will receive itemized monthly statements from us detailing the services rendered, along with the corresponding fees and expenses. This amount will be deducted from the retainer, and you will be expected to pay any fees and expenses incurred which exceed the balance of your retainer. Any bills in excess of the retainer that are not paid within sixty days will be assessed an interest charge of 1.5% per month. At the conclusion of our work, any funds remaining in your retainer account will be refunded to you.

If the terms of this letter are acceptable to you, please sign below to indicate that you have read and understand this letter and that you agree to its terms. Then please return the original signed and dated letter to me along with your check for the retainer.

I look forward to working with you and [Company Name]. If you have any questions, please give me a call.

Sincerely,

Law Firm

Lawyer Name

AGREED TO:

_____, Inc.

Dated:_____

CHAPTER 2

LETTERS FOR LITIGATORS

11. Retention Letter – Time Billing – Retainer – Evergreen

Date

Name
Company Name
Address 1
Address 2
City, State, Zip Code

Re:

Dear _____:

The purpose of this letter is to introduce our clients to the billing policies and procedures of [Firm Name].

<u>Hourly Rate:</u> The client will be billed for services rendered at the firm's hourly rate in effect at the time the work is performed. In the event of a change in rate that exceeds the initial rate billed to the client by more than ten percent (10%), the client, upon payment in full of all disbursements incurred and all fees earned, may terminate this Agreement. The hourly rates presently in effect are Principal at [$____], Associate at [$____], and Paralegal at [$____]. Our time is billed in increments of no less than six (6) minutes.

<u>Initial Consultations:</u> All initial consultations are billed at the rate of [$____] per hour, but in no instance will the charge for a consultation be less than [$____]. The initial consultation must be paid for when it is concluded.

<u>Services Rendered:</u> All services performed in connection with a matter are billed as part of that matter, including phone calls and review of correspondences.

<u>Retainers:</u> It is the policy of our office to request from each client after the initial consultation a retainer in connection with the matter in question. The parties agree that the retainer in this matter shall be [$____]. Until the retainer is paid in full, no services will be performed on your behalf by this office. To the extent that a retainer is more or less than the amount of time and disbursements expended by the attorney, the difference will be refunded or billed, as appropriate, to the client.

Replenishment of Retainer: The client agrees that whenever the amount of the retainer held by the firm falls below [$____], the client shall, **within fourteen (14) days**, replenish the retainer to the amount of [$____]. The parties agree that the firm may terminate this Agreement and withdraw its representation of the client if the client refuses or is unable to replenish the retainer in compliance with this paragraph. In the event that services are terminated pursuant to this paragraph, the firm shall return to the client the amount of the retainer that remains, if any, after accounting for all outstanding fees and disbursements, or, if the retainer is exhausted, the client shall pay all disbursements and fees owed or incurred as provided in the following paragraphs.

Disbursements: All disbursements incurred in connection with any matter are billed directly to you. Such out-of-pocket disbursements are in addition to any amounts owed to us for our fee.

Professional Statements for Services Rendered: On the first day of each month, you will receive a statement that indicates our fee for services rendered during the previous month, as well as all out-of-pocket disbursements incurred. All amounts reflected on the statement are due and payable upon receipt by you. We reserve the right without further notice to charge interest on any outstanding balances past due [__] days at [__]% per annum, and/or terminate all future services to be rendered in connection with your matter. A client may terminate this Agreement at any time, whereupon he must pay in full all disbursements incurred and all fees earned, whether accrued or outstanding. We reserve the right to send interim bills to you any time the outstanding amount on your statement for services rendered equals or exceeds [$____]. We further reserve all rights regarding the failure to pay same as we do on our regular monthly statements.

Client Files: It is the policy of this office to retain files for a period of seven (7) years from the date that your matter is resolved. Six months after your matter is resolved, your records will be placed in a storage facility, and there will be a charge (from the storage facility) to retrieve your records should the need arise.

If you have any questions concerning anything contained in this letter, please do not hesitate to ask the attorney in charge at the beginning of the initial consultation.

If after reading this letter you still wish to proceed with the initial consultation and/or to retain the services of our firm in connection with your matter, please indicate below that you have received this statement, read and understood it, and that you agree with all its terms and conditions by signing your name in full on the line provided below and dating same in the space provided. Please make all checks payable to [Firm Name].

CHAPTER 2
LETTERS FOR LITIGATORS

Please understand that unless this Agreement is signed and received by the firm, no work can be done in connection with your matter.

                Sincerely,

                Law Firm

                Lawyer Name

I/We acknowledge receipt of, have read and understand the above letter and agree to its terms and conditions set forth above.

_____   _____
CLIENT NAME   CLIENT NAME

_____   _____
Address   Address

_____   _____
City/Town, State and Zip   City/Town, State and Zip

_____   _____
Tel. No. (Home)   Tel. No. (Home)

Dated:_____   Dated:_____

12. Retention Letter – Time Billing – No Retainer

Date

Name
Company Name
Address 1
Address 2
City, State, Zip Code

    Re:

Dear _____:

Thank you for asking this firm to represent you in connection with the above matter. It was a pleasure meeting with you on [Date], and I hope we can bring this matter to a swift and favorable conclusion. I am writing to set forth our agreement regarding the terms and conditions of this Law Firm's representation of you, including our fees and services to be provided.

This firm will represent you at the rate of [$_____] per hour for all work performed by myself or any other attorney in the firm, including but not limited to legal research, preparation of correspondence or court papers, conferences, telephone calls, attendance at meetings and court proceedings, and travel time. In addition, the firm will bill you for reimbursement of all significant out-of-pocket expenses incurred in connection with this matter, including but not limited to court filing fees, subpoena costs, overnight and hand-delivery fees, and transcripts. We will assume all costs for incidental expenses such as photocopying of documents, telephone toll calls, telefaxing, and postage.

We have agreed to waive our usual requirement of a retainer prior to commencing our services. We will send you itemized monthly statements detailing our services rendered and the corresponding fees and expenses. All invoices are due and payable within thirty (30) days. Any invoices that are not paid within sixty days will be assessed an interest charge of 1.5% per month.

If the terms of this letter are agreeable to you, please sign below to indicate that you have read and understand this letter and that you agree to its terms. Please return the original signed and dated representation letter to me.

I look forward to working with you. If you have any questions, please do not hesitate to contact me.

        Sincerely,

        Law Firm

        Lawyer Name

AGREED TO:

_____

[Name]

Dated: _____

13. Retention Letter – Contingency Fee – Local Counsel

Date

Name
Company Name
Address 1
Address 2
City, State, Zip Code

Re:

Dear _____:

We received your packet for filing in the above-captioned matter.

Please allow this to confirm that I will serve as co-counsel in regard to this matter. Rule 1.5 of the Maryland Rules of Professional Conduct requires any contingent fee agreement to be in writing. It also prohibits lawyers not in the same office from sharing a fee <u>unless</u>:

1) the division of fee is in proportion to the services performed by each lawyer, or, by <u>written agreement</u> with the client, each lawyer assumes joint responsibility for the representation;

2) the client is advised of and does not object to the participation of all the lawyers involved; and

3) the total fee is reasonable.

A copy of the rule is attached.

Accordingly, our fee must be based on the proportion of services provided by each of us, or we must have a written agreement with the client that we assume joint representation. So, for example, if we divide the fee 10%/90%, we must work in that proportion or we must both assume joint liability for the case by written agreement with the client. Please confirm that your written agreement with the client complies with this.

Also, please forward us a check in the amount of three hundred five dollars ($305.00) to cover the cost of the filing and private process server fees. The filing fee is $110.00 plus $20.00 to enter your appearance as counsel for

each case, and the private process server fee is a total of $45.00 to serve both writs of summons on the same defendant.

        Sincerely,

        Law Firm

        Lawyer Name

Enclosures

14. Retention Letter – Hourly/Retainer

CHAPTER 2
Retention

Date

Name
Company Name
Address 1
Address 2
City, State, Zip Code

Re:

Dear _____:

This will confirm our agreement whereby you have hired [Firm Name] ("the Firm") to represent [Client Name] ("the Client") in connection with the above-referenced matter.

The Firm has agreed to provide legal services in connection with this matter and to keep you informed of all significant developments. You have agreed to provide the Firm with a retainer in the amount of [$_____]. We have agreed that the Client will pay fees according to the following schedule:

Partners	$325 per hour
Associates	$150-$225 per hour
Paralegal/Law Clerks	$75-$100 per hour

We review our rates annually, and the rates quoted above may be subject to change at the end of any calendar year. In addition to the rates set forth above, the Client will also be responsible for reasonable costs, including but not limited to investigative costs, expert witness fees, court and stenographers' fees, and out-of-state travel expenses. At this time, it is impossible to estimate the total cost for legal services to be provided.

Statements are issued by the Firm on a monthly basis and are due and payable within 14 days of receipt. If trial in this matter commences, fees and costs will be billed on a weekly basis. Statements will then be due and payable within three days of receipt.

You should be aware that if the Client fails to honor its payment obligations, the Firm shall be entitled to perform the minimum legal services necessary to protect the Client's interests and may elect to withdraw from our representation in the above-referenced matter. Further, by signing this agreement, the Client makes the commitment that it will be truthful with the Firm and assist the Firm in the preparation of its defense. Its failure to do so may also result in the Firm's withdrawal.

We can make no promise or guaranty as to successful resolution or eventual outcome in this matter. However, the Firm owes the Client the highest duty of advocacy permissible within the Canon of Ethics, will at all times endeavor to give it the best advice under all circumstances, and will work diligently on its behalf.

If there is anything about this agreement you do not understand, please contact me immediately. Otherwise, please sign and date this fee agreement letter and return it to me, with a retainer check in the amount of [$_____], at your earliest convenience. Once the Firm receives your check, we will begin working on this matter. We look forward to working with you.

                    Sincerely,

                    Law Firm

                    Lawyer Name

_____

Client's Signature

_____

Date

15. Retention Letter – Flat Fee Agreement Letter

CHAPTER 2
Retention

Date

Name
Company Name
Address 1
Address 2
City, State, Zip Code

Re:

Dear _____:

This will confirm our agreement whereby you have hired [Firm Name] ("the Firm") to represent you in connection with the above-referenced matter.

The Firm has agreed to provide legal services in connection with this matter and to keep you informed of all significant developments. We have agreed to a fixed fee in the amount of [$_____]. In consideration of this fee, the Firm agrees to prepare all appropriate pretrial motions, conduct reasonable investigations, and will try the case, or settle it by way of an acceptable plea bargain. This agreement does not provide for continued representation after trial, nor does it apply to retrials or appeals. You must make separate arrangements in the event of a retrial or appeals.

You will also be responsible for all costs in excess of the cumulative amount of $1,000, including such out-of-pocket disbursements as travel expenses, expert witnesses and investigators.

The Firm can make no promise or guaranty as to the successful resolution or eventual outcome of our representation of you in this matter. However, the Firm owes you the highest duty of advocacy permissible within the Canons of Ethics, will at all times endeavor to give you the best advice under all circumstances, and will work diligently on your behalf.

If there is anything about this agreement you do not understand, please contact me immediately. Otherwise, please sign and date the enclosed copy of this fee agreement letter and return it to me, along with payment in full of your fee. Once I receive payment of the fee, I will begin work on this matter.

Agreed to this _____ day of _____, 200_

By: _____
   [Client Name]

16. Retention Letter – Contingent Fee Agreement

Date

Name
Company Name
Address 1
Address 2
City, State, Zip Code

Re:

Dear _____:

[Client Name], [Client Address] ("the Client"), retains [Firm Name], [Firm Address] ("the Firm"), to perform the legal services mentioned in Paragraph One (1) below. The Firm agrees to perform them faithfully and with due diligence.

(1) The claim, controversy, and other matter with reference to which the services are to be performed are: [description of matter]

(2) The contingency upon which compensation is to be paid is the recovery of money on account of said damages.

(3) The Client will pay reasonable compensation on the foregoing contingency to the Attorney in the amount of thirty-three and one-third percent (33-1/3%) of the net amount collected, which is the amount collected after deduction of the Firm's expenses and medical liens.

(4) The Client is in any event to be liable to the Firm for its reasonable expenses and disbursements.

This agreement and its performance are subject to Rule 3:05 of the Supreme Judicial Court of Massachusetts.

WE HAVE EACH READ THE ABOVE AGREEMENT BEFORE SIGNING IT.

Witnesses to signatures:

To Client:

_____   _____
                                 [CLIENT]

To Attorney:

_____   _____
                                 [ATTORNEY]

17. Retention Letter – Expert

Date

Name
Company Name
Address 1
Address 2
City, State, Zip Code

    Re:

Dear _____:

Per our recent discussion, please contact me within the next ten days to advise of your thoughts concerning the transcript of the deposition of our client, [Client Name]. Also enclosed are copies of transcripts of the other persons deposed in this case. Our deposition of the plaintiff is tentatively scheduled for [Date].

Also, pursuant to our discussion, we will be compensating you at your hourly rate of [$_____].

Your attention to this matter is very much appreciated. Thank you.

                      Sincerely,

                      Law Firm

                      Lawyer Name

Enclosures

18. Retention Letter – Co-Counsel

Date

Name
Company Name
Address 1
Address 2
City, State, Zip Code

Re:

Dear _____:

I am in receipt of the transcript of judgment you sent.

In order to begin work on this matter, I will need a retainer of $1,000. This should cover the recording of the judgment in Anne County and service of a garnishment and writ of execution on the judgment debtor. My hourly rate for these services is $300, and the filing fees will probably be less than $100. It will be necessary to keep a minimum balance of $500.00 in escrow.

Of course, should we strike paydirt, any unearned funds on deposit will be promptly refunded.

Sincerely,

Law Firm

Lawyer Name

B. Declination Letters

1. Declination Letter – Contingent Fee – Employment

Date

<u>VIA CERTIFIED MAIL, RETURN RECEIPT REQUESTED</u>

Name
Company Name
Address 1
Address 2
City, State, Zip Code

Re:

Dear _____:

It was a pleasure for [Associate Name] and me to meet with you in our office on [Date] and again on [Date] to discuss your potential case against [Defendant Name]. Please allow this letter to confirm our discussion. Having considered all the information available to us at this time, and after my having attended the unemployment hearing with you here in [City] on [Date], and having obtained and reviewed the papers [Defendant Name] unsuccessfully attempted to introduce into evidence at that hearing (copies of which I gave you on [Date] after the hearing), we have reluctantly concluded that we cannot represent you in this matter on a contingent-fee basis. From our decision, you should not conclude that you do not have a cause of action. Our decision not to represent you does not imply or express any advice about whether you do or do not have a case. <u>It only means that, in our opinion, any likely recovery in this case would not justify the time and resources we would have to invest to obtain it</u>. It is possible that another lawyer or law firm would feel differently and would be willing to undertake this matter on a contingent-fee basis.

Because the law imposes certain time limits on when claims and suits may be filed ("statutes of limitation"), your right to file a claim or suit will expire with the passage of time. These deadlines may begin to expire very soon, as you learned when you visited the EEOC here in [City] on [Date] and were told of their timetable for filing a claim. Subject to a few exceptions, lawsuits for libel and slander in Maryland will usually be barred if not filed within one year. Suits for other causes of action in Maryland may have longer statutes of limitation. You should not delay in pursuing legal action if you intend to do so, because your claim or suit—no matter what it is for—will be barred if not filed within the applicable statute of limitations for that particular cause of action.

As I promised at our last meeting, I will send you a copy of anything I receive from the Maryland Office of Unemployment Insurance so that you can take the necessary steps to protect your rights in that regard. We wish you every success in the future. Please don't hesitate to call if we can be of assistance.

        Sincerely,

        Law Firm

        Lawyer Name

2. Declination Letter – Contingent Fee – General

Date

Name
Company Name
Address 1
Address 2
City, State, Zip Code

Re:

Dear _____:

This is in follow-up to our telephone conversation yesterday regarding the materials you forwarded to me last month. While it does appear that some of the terms of the contract between you and the above-referenced persons may have been breached, in my opinion, this alone would not justify filing a contingent-fee lawsuit unless a) the amount of quantifiable and reasonably certain damages is sufficient to warrant the expenditure of resources necessary to prosecute the action, and b) the responsible parties have the resources to pay a judgment.

From what you told me on the phone, it does not appear that the damage amounts are substantial or provable, and I therefore will not be able to represent you in this matter unless you are able to provide additional facts substantiating and quantifying your damages. This is only my opinion; other attorneys might reach different conclusions. My unwillingness to take this case without further documentation and information does not mean you do not have a case—only that I am not able to undertake it on a contingent-fee basis.

I have not reviewed or analyzed your documents for the purposes of determining what state's law would apply or where suit should be filed. Nor have I attempted to make a determination about when the statute of limitations would expire in this matter, or whether it has already expired. If you wish to pursue this matter, you should either seek other counsel or provide me with detailed support for a claim of monetary harm as soon as possible, because your right to file suit will expire with the passage of time, if it has not already.

Sincerely,

Law Firm

Lawyer Name

CHAPTER 2
LETTERS FOR LITIGATORS

3. Declination Letter – Contingent Fee – Whistleblower Specific

Date

Name
Company Name
Address 1
Address 2
City, State, Zip Code

Re:

Dear _____:

It was a pleasure meeting you yesterday. I have read the materials you left with me, as well as the two pages you faxed.

My understanding is that you believe some co-workers may be falsifying time records, and that you reported this to your superiors and are now the target of retaliation, which is prohibited by the terms of the company handbook. You indicated you have copies of time records and schedules that document the fact that the time cards are false.

My practice focuses on representing whistleblowers who bring suits under the federal civil false claims act. As we discussed briefly yesterday in our meeting, in order to bring a case under this statute, you must have evidence or knowledge that someone has <u>knowingly submitted a false claim to the federal government</u>.

Because your situation does not appear to involve any federal funds, it does not fall within the scope of the civil false claims act. There are other potential legal remedies you may have, but since my practice in the employment area is limited to false claims act suits, I cannot assist you in any of these other areas. Instead, I suggest you consult an attorney who handles employment law issues. You may be able to obtain names of employment lawyers from the Lawyer Referral Service of the Bar Association of [City]. As I am sure you know, your right to file a claim or lawsuit will expire with the passage of time, and you should therefore not delay in retaining a lawyer.

I wish you success in resolving this matter.

Sincerely,

Law Firm

Lawyer Name

4. Declination Letter – Contingent Fee – Whistleblower General

Date

Name
Company Name
Address 1
Address 2
City, State, Zip Code

Re:

Dear _____:

After reviewing the materials you sent me and researching the applicable law, I have determined, regrettably, that I cannot undertake your representation.

Decisions about whether to take a case are difficult and involve such factors as my commitments to other clients, the complexity of the case, the potential for recovery in a case, and many others. From the facts you have given me, it does appear that there may have been fraud on the government by one or more defendants. However, I am not in a position to supply the effort and time that would be required to pursue this case. From my decision, you should not conclude that you do not have a cause of action. My decision not to represent you does not imply or express any advice about whether you do or do not have a case.

Because the law imposes certain time limits on when claims may be filed, your legal right to file a claim may expire with the passage of time. The false claims act statute of limitations provides that a *qui tam* action may not be brought after the later of a) more than six years after the date on which the false claim is made, or b) more than three years after the date when facts material to the right of action are known or reasonably should have been known by the official of the U.S. charged with responsibility to act in the circumstances, but in no event more than 10 years after the date on which the violation is committed. Accordingly, if you have any intentions of filing a claim or lawsuit regarding this matter, you should contact the attorney of your choice at once; otherwise, your claim or suit may be barred.

Sincerely,

Law Firm

Lawyer Name

5. Declination Letter – Contingent Fee – Medical Malpractice General

CHAPTER 2
Retention

Date

VIA CERTIFIED MAIL
RETURN RECEIPT REQUESTED AND VIA FIRST CLASS MAIL

Name
Company Name
Address 1
Address 2
City, State, Zip Code

Re:

Dear _____:

This is in follow-up to our meeting on [Date] regarding your potential medical malpractice case against [First Doctor's Name] for prescribing oral contraceptives despite the fact that they were contraindicated.

Since our meeting, I have reviewed some of your medical records as well as some of the medical literature on oral contraceptives, and I have spoken with two expert witness locator services.

As you know from my previous correspondence, locating and hiring an expert witness can be costly. You did not want to invest the funds for the search process if we could get the same information and testimony from the physician who treated you for the [condition alleged to have been caused by the medical negligence], [Second Doctor's Name]. Accordingly, on [Date], I asked him whether the oral contraceptives prescribed by [First Doctor's Name] caused or contributed to your [condition alleged to have been caused by the medical negligence]; his response was that they did not.

Now, this is only his opinion. It is possible 1) that he could change his mind or 2) that we could find another expert who will testify that they did.

However, having considered all the information available to me at this time, I have reluctantly concluded that I cannot represent you. Decisions about whether to take a case are difficult and involve many factors ranging from

CHAPTER 2

LETTERS FOR LITIGATORS

my commitments to other clients to the potential for recovery in a given case. From my decision, you should not conclude that you do not have a cause of action. My decision not to represent you does not imply or express any advice about whether you do or do not have a case. It only means that, in my opinion, any likely recovery in this case would not justify the time and resources I would have to invest to obtain it.

Because the law imposes certain time limits on when claims may be filed, your right to file a claim may expire with the passage of time. Accordingly, if you have any intentions of filing a claim or lawsuit regarding this matter, you should contact another attorney of your choice at once; otherwise, your claim or suit may be barred.

I wish you every success in pursuing this matter, and, at your request, I will provide copies of your file to any attorney you may designate.

                Sincerely,

                Law Firm

                Lawyer Name

6. Declination Letter – Contingent Fee – Medical Malpractice Specific

CHAPTER 2
Retention

Date

VIA CERTIFIED MAIL, RETURN RECEIPT REQUESTED

Name
Company Name
Address 1
Address 2
City, State, Zip Code

Re:

Dear _____:

I have received and reviewed the documents you sent on [Date] and discussed with my assistant, [Assistant's Name], the information you gave her on the phone today, including the fact that the operation in which the alleged malpractice occurred was [Date].

The statute of limitations in [State] provides that suit must be brought within [Number of Years] of the malpractice, or within [Number of Years] of when it was discovered, whichever is earlier. In order to avoid having to fight with the defendant over the issue of when you first discovered it, suit needs to be filed within [Number] years of when you had the operation.

I do not know whether the non-fusion was caused by [Doctor's Name]'s breach of the applicable standard of care. It may be that fusions don't always work, through no fault of the doctor. In order to pursue a medical negligence claim, we must have a doctor who will testify that [Doctor's Name] did breach the standard of care. It is my understanding that you do not have any doctor willing to say that, at this point. Thus, if we are to proceed, I would need to find such a doctor. To do this, I would need to have the documentation from that surgery (operative notes, etc.), which has not been supplied to me. Then I would need to submit all your records to one or more experts for review to determine whether [Doctor's Name]'s care fell below the applicable standard of care. Doctors charge a substantial amount of money to do these record reviews, and they can take a long time to do them.

The expert would also need to state that the non-fusion caused damage to you. Your medical records go into detail about numerous problems, and it

CHAPTER 2
LETTERS FOR LITIGATORS

may be difficult to find someone who can separate out all the medical issues and state to a reasonable degree of medical probability that [Doctor's Name] did something wrong which caused some or all of your problems.

Not only will it be time-consuming, but it will also be expensive, probably in the range of $5,000, to find such an expert. This, coupled with the very short period of time left in which to locate the expert, makes me unable to take on your case. This does not mean you do not have a case. You should definitely try to find another lawyer, and you must do so immediately, because of the statute of limitations problem described above. I wish I could be of more assistance, but because of the time urgency and my existing commitments to other clients, regrettably, I cannot. I wish you good luck in pursuing this, and in finding good medical care to help resolve the problems.

Please let me know if you would like me to forward any or all of your records to another attorney, or to you, and I will do so immediately.

Sincerely,

Law Firm

Lawyer Name

7. Declination Letter – Contingent Fee – Negligence

CHAPTER 2
Retention

Date

VIA CERTIFIED MAIL, RETURN RECEIPT REQUESTED AND FIRST CLASS MAIL

Name
Company Name
Address 1
Address 2
City, State, Zip Code

    Re:

Dear _____:

After reviewing the materials you sent me, investigating, and researching the applicable law, I have determined, regrettably, that I cannot undertake your representation in connection with the fire of [Date] that claimed your daughter's life.

Decisions about whether to take a case are difficult and involve such factors as my commitments to other clients, the complexity of the case, the potential for recovery in a case, and many others. From the facts you have given me, it does appear that there may have been negligence or other wrongful conduct by one or more defendants (including the sofa manufacturer, the sofa deliverer, the sofa packager, the boys who set the fire, the parent(s) of the boys, and possibly others) that could result in a recovery to you. However, because of the complexity of the issues and the uncertainty surrounding whether there is insurance coverage that would pay a judgment, together with the fact that the sofa manufacturer may be out of business, I am not in a position to supply the effort and time that would be required to pursue this case. My concern is that even after spending the necessary sums to take this case through litigation, there may be no insurance coverage from which to collect any verdict that might be awarded in your favor.

From my decision, you should not conclude that you do not have a cause of action. My decision only means that I am unable to undertake this case. However, there are many other attorneys who may evaluate this matter differently and who might be willing to take your case.

Because the law imposes certain time limits on when claims may be filed, your legal right to file a claim will expire with the passage of time. A negligence action must be brought before the expiration of [applicable number] years from when the [triggering event] occurred. Accordingly, if you have any intentions of filing a claim or lawsuit regarding this matter, you should contact another attorney at once; otherwise, your right to sue will expire as stated above.

Sincerely,

Law Firm

Lawyer Name

C. Billing Letters

1. Billing Letter – Cover Letter

Date

Name
Company Name
Address 1
Address 2
City, State, Zip Code

    Re:

Dear _____:

Enclosed herewith please find my invoice showing itemization of fees and expenses to date, together with a statement applying your $350.00 retainer, for a balance due of $40.00.

Please make check payable to [Firm Name].

                                Sincerely,

                                Law Firm

                                Lawyer Name

Enclosures

2. Billing Letter – Payment Plan

Date

Name
Company Name
Address 1
Address 2
City, State, Zip Code

Re:

Dear _____:

Enclosed is your June invoice, which reflects your past due balance.

This letter will confirm the agreement we reached in our telephone conversation today that you will make monthly payments in the amount of [$____] for the next six months to retire your outstanding balance to this firm of [$____].

I have agreed to this payment plan in an effort to ease your financial burden, and have agreed to waive interest charges so long as you continue to make your monthly payments as agreed herein. As such, I hope you will make every effort to retire this balance in a timely fashion in accordance with our agreement.

I hope all is well with you, and that the store enjoys continued growth and success in your new location.

Sincerely,

Law Firm

Lawyer Name

3. Billing Letter – Collection

Date

Name
Company Name
Address 1
Address 2
City, State, Zip Code

    Re:

Dear _____:

Recently, my partners voted to compel me to file a motion to withdraw from your case, and to initiate a collection action against you for the outstanding balance on your bill, unless you contact me next week and we are able to identify our dispute (if any) and resolve it. It is difficult to argue against this vote, because you have promised to make a payment at least twice and have not done so, and now you do not even extend to me the courtesy of returning my calls.

It really puzzles me as to why you have been so unresponsive. I have always given your cases priority over my other clients by making myself available to represent both of you in various matters whenever the need arose. Unilaterally, I have reduced our past bills due to our friendship. Now we are close to resolving your divorce and we find ourselves in this difficult situation.

Please call me immediately so that we can amicably resolve this problem. I would certainly consider any hardship you might be experiencing. Your call would be much appreciated. Thank you.

                        Sincerely,

                        Law Firm

                        Lawyer Name

4. Billing Letter – Evergreen

Date

Name
Company Name
Address 1
Address 2
City, State, Zip Code

Re:

Dear _____:

Enclosed is [Judge's Name]'s Amended Order requiring [Defendant's Name] to come in for examination in aid of execution on June 28, provided I am able to serve him with the Order by June 18. Please provide me with any information you may have regarding [Defendant's Name]'s whereabouts, or any other identifying information, to facilitate the process of locating and serving him with the Order.

I plan to ask the standard assets and liabilities questions at the examination, but ask that if you have any particular topics you would like me to pursue, please let me know as soon as possible.

Enclosed is my bill for services rendered, less credits already on deposit, together with a request that the retainer be replenished to reach the agreed minimum, for a total payment of [$_____], which I anticipate will cover all or most of the examination in aid of execution as well as the costs to have [Defendant's Name] served with the Order requiring his appearance.

Please feel free to contact me with any questions or comments.

Sincerely,

Law Firm

Lawyer Name

5. Billing Letter – Request for Client to Advance Expenses

Date

Name
Company Name
Address 1
Address 2
City, State, Zip Code

Re:

Dear _____:

The filing fee in the above-referenced matter is [$_____], and the private process server fee for all defendants totals [$_____]. Time is of the essence; as you know, we have a statute of limitations date of [Date]. Please provide us with a check in the amount of [$_____] to cover the cost of the fees at your earliest convenience.

We will be providing you with a draft complaint for your review within the week.

Sincerely,

Law Firm

Lawyer Name

D. Withdrawing Representation

1. Withdrawal – General

Date

VIA CERTIFIED MAIL, RETURN RECEIPT REQUESTED, RESTRICTED DELIVERY

Name
Company Name
Address 1
Address 2
City, State, Zip Code

    Re:

Dear _____:

Pursuant to paragraph 5 of our fee agreement, which provides that _____, I am withdrawing as your attorney in this case.

As you know, the law provides that a negligence action must be brought before the expiration of three years from when the negligence occurred. You should therefore contact another attorney of your choice to represent you well in advance of the expiration of this period.

                  Sincerely,

                  Law Firm

                  Lawyer Name

2. Withdrawal – Contingency Fee

Date

VIA CERTIFIED MAIL, RETURN RECEIPT REQUESTED, RESTRICTED DELIVERY

Name
Company Name
Address 1
Address 2
City, State, Zip Code

   Re:

Dear _____:

After careful thought, investigation, research, and deliberation, we have made a decision at our office that [Firm Name] will no longer be able to represent you regarding the above-referenced matter.

Our decision not to handle your case is based, among other reasons, upon a financial and economic reality. It is very expensive to bring a case to court and to trial. This expense is borne by both you and our Law Firm. It is our professional opinion that the economic cost to bring this claim is not justified by the potential value of a judgment or verdict in your favor.

You may have your case reviewed by another attorney, and I encourage you to do so, because another attorney may view the information differently. Please be advised, however, that, by law, *you have no more than three years* from the date of [Injured Party's Name]'s death to file a complaint, if you choose to proceed. Your file will be forwarded to you at your request.

If you have other questions or concerns, I encourage you to contact me so that I may discuss them with you.

                Sincerely,

                Law Firm

                Lawyer Name

CHAPTER 3

Demand

Settlement is almost universally viewed as the preferred result in litigation because it prevents litigation, or resolves it on terms the parties can live with. A well-written demand letter can make the difference between a case tried and a case settled. Not only does a demand letter communicate your client's terms and conditions to the other side, but it showcases the strength of your case and lets the opposition know how well-prepared you are. Early drafting of a demand letter, even if it is not sent at the time, can help focus discovery and trial preparation, and burst the bubble of unrealistic expectations should they exist.

Exercise care and restraint when sending pre-suit demand letters to avoid becoming a target of a defamation or intentional infliction suit. As discussed in the Introduction to this book, the litigation privilege may protect communications made during litigation, but communications made preliminary to litigation may not be protected unless the writer is seriously considering judicial proceedings in good faith. A failure to follow through on a pre-litigation threat to sue may give rise to the claim that the threats were not made in good faith. Avoid threats of criminal prosecution, as the rules of professional conduct in many jurisdictions forbid a lawyer from threatening to present criminal charges solely to obtain an advantage in a private civil matter.

A. Demands

1. Demand Letter – Consumer Protection

Date

VIA CERTIFIED MAIL

Name
Company Name
Address 1
Address 2
City, State, Zip Code

Re:

Dear _____:

This law firm represents [Client Name] in connection with claims against [Company Name] for breach of contract, fraud, misrepresentation, and violations of the Massachusetts Consumer Protection Act, M.G.L. c. 93A, in connection with certain agreements between you and [Client Name] relative to proposed landscaping work for the premises noted above.

In [Month, Year] [Client Name] retained you to perform landscaping work at their home. From late [Date] through mid-[Month], you performed certain services, for which [Client Name] paid you the sum of [$_____].

In [Month, Year], you presented [Client Name] with a proposal for additional landscaping services, which you estimated at a cost of [$_____]. At that time, [Client Name] agreed to your proposal and provided you with a deposit toward those services in the amount of [$_____]. Shortly after receiving [Client Name]'s money, you stated that the work had to be postponed until [Month, Year] because one of your employees was ill.

In [Month, Year], you informed [Client Name], for the first time, that you had neglected to invoice them for services you allegedly rendered during the previous year in the amount of approximately [$_____]. You also stated that there would be a "design fee" of [$_____] for landscape design time which was never previously disclosed by you or agreed to by the [Client Name]. You also informed [Client Name] that the cost of their seasonal maintenance would increase from [$_____] per year to [$_____] per year. The [Client Name] was unaware of any of these costs prior to this discussion. At that time, [Client Name] protested these undisclosed charges, and you agreed to waive the "design fee" and reimburse [Client Name] the sum of [$_____] from the original amount they had paid. In subsequent conversations with [Client Name], you again agreed that the sum of [$_____] would be refunded. As of this date, [Client Name] has not received that refund from you, and their numerous telephone calls to you have never been returned.

CHAPTER 3

Demand

In [Month, Year], [Client Name] informed you that they were terminating their relationship with you. At that point, they had given you a deposit of [$_____] for landscaping services to be performed in [Year], which you have never performed. [Client Name] has made numerous attempts to contact you; however, you have repeatedly failed to return their telephone calls.

Your conduct set forth above constitutes a breach of the agreements between you and [Client Name], as well as fraud, misrepresentation, unjust enrichment and a violation of the Massachusetts Consumer Protection Act, M.G.L. c. 93A. Pursuant to M.G.L. c. 93A, you have thirty (30) days to respond to this letter with a reasonable offer of settlement. If you do not respond within that time, you may be found liable for multiple damages, court costs and attorneys' fees.

On behalf of [Client Name], demand is hereby made for immediate payment of [$_____]. If payment in that amount is not received by this office on or before [Date], we will institute litigation against you and will seek all available legal and equitable remedies, including but not limited to treble damages, court costs and attorneys' fees pursuant to M.G.L. c. 93A, and all other remedies available to the [Client Name] under applicable law. In addition, we will take appropriate measures to report your conduct to the Better Business Bureau, the Attorney General's office, state and local licensing and consumer protection agencies, and other governmental authorities.

Sincerely,

Law Firm

Lawyer Name

2. Demand Letter – Lease

Date

VIA CERTIFIED MAIL AND FIRST CLASS MAIL

Name
Company Name
Address 1
Address 2
City, State, Zip Code

Re:

Dear _____:

This Law Firm represents [Client Name] in connection with a Lease Agreement ("Lease") with [Lessor Name] dated [Date]. [Lessor Name] is currently in default under the Lease for the above-captioned property for failure to pay rent, taxes, maintenance charges, late fees and other expenses due thereunder from [Dates] in the aggregate amount of [$_____]. A copy of the Profile History List, which sets forth the breakdown for the amounts currently due (exclusive of interest), is attached hereto as Appendix A.

The Lease provides for payment of rent, taxes and other applicable charges on or before the first day of each calendar month. [Lessor Name] has failed to timely pay amounts due under the Lease and is currently in default thereof. Please be advised that unless full payment in the amount of [$_____] is received by [Client Name] within ten (10) days of the date of this letter, this Law Firm will commence immediate eviction proceedings against [Lessor Name], re-enter the premises, and exercise all other available legal and equitable remedies, including but not limited to seeking interest, court costs and attorneys' fees.

In order to avoid eviction and litigation proceedings, demand is hereby made for you to remit immediate payment in full to [Client Name] within ten (10) days. Payment should be sent to [Client Name/Address].

If you have any questions, please do not hesitate to contact me.

>Sincerely,

>Law Firm

>Lawyer Name

cc: Client

3. Demand Letter – Contract Nonpayment

Date

<u>VIA CERTIFIED AND FIRST CLASS MAIL</u>

Name
Company Name
Address 1
Address 2
City, State, Zip Code

    Re:

Dear _____:

This Law Firm represents [Client Name] in connection with claims against [Company Name] for breach of contract, unfair and deceptive business practices, and related claims arising from [Company Name]'s failure to pay [Client Name] for services rendered in the amount of [$_____].

As you know, [Client Name] and [Company Name] entered into a Master Services Agreement dated [Date]. Pursuant to that Agreement, [Client Name] performed custom software development services for [Company Name], for which [Company Name] is obligated to pay [Client Name] within thirty (30) days from the date of invoice.

In [Month, Year], [Client Name] completed the required services under the contract, and on [Date], sent [Company Name] a final invoice in the amount of [$_____] for services rendered. At no time did [Company Name] reject [Client Name]'s services, or otherwise indicate that [Client Name] did not perform its obligations under the contract. In [Month, Year], [Company Name] made a partial payment of [$_____] toward the final invoice, leaving a remaining balance due of [$_____]. Since that time, [Company Name] has failed or refused to make any further payment, despite numerous telephone calls from, and "past-due" invoices sent by, [Client Name], copies of which are attached.

The actions of [Company Name] in failing to pay [Client Name] amounts due and owing for services rendered constitutes a breach of the agreement between [Company Name] and [Client Name], as well as a violation of the Massachusetts Unfair Business Practices Act, G.L. c. 93A.

Demand is hereby made for immediate payment of [$_____] to [Client Name]. Please be advised that unless such payment is received by this office on or before [Date], we will commence litigation against [Company Name] to seek appropriate damages, including seeking multiple damages, interest, court costs and attorneys' fees. [Client Name] will also forward information regarding this matter to the appropriate credit-reporting agencies.

If you have any questions, please do not hesitate to contact me.

Sincerely,

Law Firm

Lawyer Name

Enclosure
cc: Client

4. Demand Letter – Professional Fees

Date

VIA CERTIFIED MAIL

Name
Company Name
Address 1
Address 2
City, State, Zip Code

Re:

Dear _____:

This Law Firm has been retained by [Client Name] to pursue legal action against you in connection with fees owed to her for professional services she rendered to you from September [Year] through April [Year] as follows:

September ____	8 visits	$ _____
October ____	9 visits	$ _____
November ____	6 visits	$ _____
December ____	6 visits	$ _____
January ____	5 visits	$ _____
February ____	6 visits	$ _____
March ____	8 visits	$ _____
April ____	8 visits	$ _____
TOTAL:		$ _____

Please note that [Client Name] received two payments from your insurance company in [Month, Year] in the total amount of [$_____], thereby reducing the balance due to [$_____].

[Client Name] has sent you invoices and has previously attempted to contact you to seek payments of the above fees, which you have failed and refused to pay. Accordingly, demand is hereby made for immediate payment of [$_____]. Please be advised that unless such payment is received by this office on or before [Date], we will institute formal legal proceedings against you for collection of the above amounts, plus payment of interest, court costs and attorneys' fees.

If you have any questions, please do not hesitate to contact me.

Sincerely,

Law Firm

Lawyer Name

cc: Client

5. Demand Letter – Business Defamation

Date

<u>VIA CERTIFIED MAIL</u>

Name
Company Name
Address 1
Address 2
City, State, Zip Code

    Re:

Dear _____:

This Law Firm represents [Client Web Developer] in connection with claims against [Defendant Company Name] for defamation, interference with contractual and business relations, and related claims arising out of certain false and misleading statements made by representatives of [Defendant Company Name] regarding [Client Web Developer] and its services. These claims arise from blatantly false and damaging statements made by [Name/Names of Defendant Representatives] that have caused [Client Web Developer] severe economic damages and harm to its business reputation.

By way of background, in [Month, Year], representatives of [Defendant Company Name] met with [Client Representative Name] to discuss the possibility of engaging [Client Web Developer] for certain web development services. Several meetings were held, which resulted in [Defendant Company Name] advising [Client Web Developer] that it was not feasible for [Client Web Developer] to undertake the project. Apparently, [Client Web Developer] was the third web site development firm with which [Defendant Company Name] was unable to formulate a design plan for its web site.

On [Date], an article appeared in the [Publication Name] regarding the difficulties in finding qualified web site developers, including problems with "missed deadlines, overshot budgets, malfunctioning sites or fly-by-night design operations." The article featured an interview with [Name of Defendant Representative]. In that article, _____ was quoted as saying, <u>inter alia</u>, that she has "yet to find a web site design firm that knows what it's doing," and that after lengthy discussions with one developer, "the firm suddenly demanded to host [Defendant Company Name]'s web site for an extra [$____] a month," that "[Defendant Company Name] had the equipment for that work already and had never discussed hosting the site," and that "[f]or a paltry $500 a month the design firm abandoned a [$_____] contract, leaving [Defendant Company Name] executives with a lot of wasted time." The article did not expressly name [Client Web Developer] as the web site developer for whom [Name of Defendant Representative] reserved "her real ire."

CHAPTER

Demand

During [Month], [Client Web Developer] was also engaged in discussions with a prospective client regarding the development of a web site with a development cost of approximately [$_____]. The prospective client saw the article in [Publication Name], and contacted [Name of Defendant Representative] to ascertain the identity of the company about which she spoke in the article. [Name of Defendant Representative] identified the company as [Client Web Developer]. During that conversation, [Name of Defendant Representative] also made further false and defamatory statements regarding [Defendant Company Name]'s relationship with [Client Web Developer], substantially impugning the reputation of [Client Web Developer]. The false statements included [Name of Defendant Representative] stating that [Defendant Company Name] had engaged [Client Web Developer] as its web site designer, was under contract with [Client web Developer], that [Client Web Developer] had breached its contract with [Defendant Company Name], that [Client Web Developer] attempted to "hold up" [Defendant Company Name] over a hosting contract, and that it had otherwise failed to meet its obligations in the development of [Defendant Company Name]'s web site. There is absolutely no truth to any of these statements, which have resulted in severe economic and business reputation damages to [Client Web Developer].

As a direct and proximate result of [Name of Defendant Representative]'s false, misleading and defamatory statements, the prospective client contacted [Client Web Developer] and stated that it decided not to engage [Client Web Developer] for the development of its web site. The prospective client specifically stated that the primary reason for its decision was a negative reference that it received from [Defendant Company Name]. Upon further inquiry, it was revealed that the source of the statements was [Name of Defendant Representative], and that [Name of Defendant Representative]'s statements were entirely false.

Based upon the foregoing, [Client Web Developer] is currently considering taking legal action against [Defendant Company Name] and [Name of Defendant Representative] individually to recover the damages it has suffered, not only through the loss of a major contract, but also for the harm to its business reputation arising from [Name of Defendant Representative]'s false statements. [Defendant Company Name] and its employees are hereby advised to cease and desist from making any further false and defamatory statements to any other individual or entity regarding

[Client Web Developer]. Any further false and defamatory statements made by [Name of Defendant Representative] or any other representative of [Defendant Company Name] will result in immediate legal action by [Client Web Developer] seeking injunctive and monetary relief against [Defendant Company Name].

In addition, [Client Web developer] hereby demands payment from [Defendant Company Name] of [$_____], representing the amount of the lost contract. If such payment is not received by [Date], [Client Web Developer] will have no choice but to consider all its legal options, including litigation seeking, among other relief, multiple damages, punitive damages and attorneys' fees.

                        Sincerely,

                        Law Firm

                        Lawyer Name

cc: Client

6. Demand Letter – Employment – Sexual Harassment

CHAPTER 3

Demand

Date

VIA CERTIFIED MAIL

Name
Company Name
Address 1
Address 2
City, State, Zip Code

Re:

Dear _____:

This Law Firm has been retained by [Client Name] in connection with claims against [Defendant Company Name] for sexual harassment, gender discrimination, constructive discharge from her employment, and related claims. As is further detailed below, [Client Name] was subjected to repeated sexual harassment and a hostile work environment by her immediate supervisor and the company [Defendant Company Name], in violation of, inter alia, 42 U.S.C. § 2000e, et seq. (Title VII), 29 C.F.R. 1604, G.L. c. 151B and 804 C.M.R. 1.00 et seq. She was also subjected to retaliation for reporting these incidents, as well as other wrongful conduct, in violation of applicable law.

Chronology of Events

[Client Name] began working for [Defendant Company Name] in [Month, Year] as the Office Manager. Her starting salary was [$_____]. Her responsibilities included creating marketing materials, organizing filing systems, customer service, technical support, filling orders, dealing with vendors, and promoting the company at conferences. After six months with the company, [Client Name] received an outstanding performance review, resulting in a thirty percent raise (to [$_____]) and a promotion to the position of Executive Coordinator for [Supervisor Name].

During the next several months, [Client Name] diligently assisted [Defendant Company Name] and [Supervisor Name] by promoting the company and coordinating _____ appearances and course materials for various conferences and events. This included traveling with [Supervisor

Name], along with in-office maintenance of [Supervisor Name] client correspondence and conference materials. During this time, various members of the _____ remarked to [Client Name] that she was performing admirably, and that she was serving well as a "buffer" between [Supervisor Name] and other [Defendant Company Name] employees with whom he had a history of conflict.

In the spring and summer of [Year], [Client Name] traveled with [Supervisor Name] to at least four different out-of-state meetings. One such meeting was a facilitation engagement held in [Month, Year] at [Facility Name] in [City, State]. During this engagement, [Supervisor Name] was participating in a "team facilitation" exercise for a group of approximately fifteen people. [Client Name] was assisting him. During the course of this exercise, [Supervisor Name] came up behind [Client Name], who was seated, and placed his hands under her hair and began rubbing the back of her neck. [Client Name] was humiliated and offended by this unprofessional and unwarranted conduct, which occurred in a room full of clients.

During the months following the [Date] meeting, [Supervisor Name] initiated several conversations with [Client Name] during which he suggested that they get together socially outside of the office. On one occasion, [Supervisor Name] stated that he wanted to take [Client Name] to a theater production. On another occasion, he asked [Client Name] if he could take her to a movie. On each occasion, [Client Name] declined these invitations, expressly stating to [Supervisor Name] that she was not interested in seeing him socially, and that she did not think it was appropriate considering their professional relationship.

In addition, [Supervisor Name] often initiated conversations with [Client Name] regarding various women he was dating, or wanted to date, stating to [Client Name] that he was dissatisfied with his relationships. On each such occasion, [Client Name] would change the subject to business matters.

In early [Month, Year], [Supervisor Name] began to completely avoid contact or communication with [Client Name]. This caused [Client Name] great distress and concern over the performance of her duties as [Supervisor Name]'s Executive Coordinator. [Supervisor Name] repeatedly avoided discussions with [Client Name] when she informed him she needed to meet with him regarding urgent business matters. As a result, [Client Name] began to question her own job performance and value to [Supervisor Name] and [Defendant Company Name].

On [Date], [Supervisor Name] and [Client Name] were in their shared office. At this time, [Client Name] informed [Supervisor Name] that she

CHAPTER 3

Demand

needed his input and approval regarding various projects she was working on. [Supervisor Name] responded that he could not discuss them with her. [Client Name] then stated that she felt [Supervisor Name] was ignoring and avoiding her, and that this was impacting her ability to properly perform her job. At this point, [Supervisor Name] closed the office door. He responded to [Client Name] "You're right, I have been avoiding you." [Client Name] inquired why he was doing this. [Supervisor Name] stated: "I often tell you about women I date, but I really haven't had any relationships with women. When I go out with women, all I do is think about you. I have trouble with any other relationships because I am only thinking about you."

[Client Name]'s response was a combination of embarrassment and outrage. She stated to [Supervisor Name] that she always felt her job at [Defendant Company Name] presented tremendous opportunity for her, and that he had created a "lose-lose" situation by his recent statements and actions. [Supervisor Name] responded by telling [Client Name], "It doesn't need to be that way. If you and I were together, you could be on the Board of Directors." [Supervisor Name] then continued by making a rambling series of statements to [Client Name], including: "You're all I think about . . . you're so beautiful . . . I just want to be with you . . . I love your blond hair . . . I melt when I see you . . . the reason I don't come into the office is because I can't function around you . . . I get turned on when I see how good you are with clients."

[Client Name] was shocked by these remarks. She felt powerless and incapable of responding. Her only statement to [Supervisor Name] was that they could not have a romantic relationship, and that they needed to devise a way to work together professionally. She suggested that they "build a wall" between them so they could communicate and work professionally. [Supervisor Name] then responded, "If you must build a wall, let it be a brick wall, not cement, so the bricks can be removed if we want them to." At this point, [Client Name] ended the discussion.

The following day, [Client Name] reported all of the above events, including each of the above statements by [Supervisor Name], to Susan Smith. She also had a discussion with you to report [Supervisor Name]'s conduct. [Client Name] informed each of you that she was fearful of any confrontation with [Supervisor Name] and believed that she was in danger of losing her job.

On [Date], [Supervisor Name] and _____ met with [Client Name]. [Supervisor Name] acknowledged and apologized for his inappropriate conduct. [Supervisor Name] then informed [Client Name] that there would be no repercussions regarding her job. [Client Name] left that meeting still extremely upset, but hopeful that the situation had been addressed and resolved by [Defendant Company Name] management, and that further incidents would not recur.

On [Date], [Supervisor Name] telephoned [Client Name] in her office. He made numerous disparaging statements regarding various individuals at [Defendant Company Name], and was critical of several recent management and personnel decisions. His tone of voice was extremely hostile, and he screamed at [Client Name] throughout the conversation. Immediately after this telephone conversation, [Client Name] came into the conference room to advise you of this conversation. As she entered your office, [Supervisor Name] called her again. When she took the call, he stated, "Everything I just told you is confidential." He further advised her that he questioned her loyalty and commitment to him, and that he felt he could not trust her because she reported the incidents of [Date] to _____. Immediately following this telephone conversation, [Client Name], believing she could no longer function as a valuable employee at [Defendant Company Name], prepared her written resignation, which she delivered to you on [Date].

On [Date], [Client Name] received a response to her resignation letter from [Defendant Company Name] management. This memo was nothing short of outrageous, as it attempted to deny previously admitted conduct by [Supervisor Name], and to shift to [Client Name] a portion of the blame for [Supervisor Name]'s illegal conduct. This memo also contains a series of false and misleading allegations about [Client Name] that were never previously raised by [Defendant Company Name] management. [Client Name] expressly denies the allegations in this memo, and considers it an act of retaliation by [Defendant Company Name] management for reporting [Supervisor Name]'s illegal conduct. Immediately upon receipt of this memo, [Client Name] informed you that she was too upset to discuss the memo, and she left for the day. The following day, she met with you and specifically denied the false charges in the October 16 memo, which she refused to sign.

During the next several weeks, [Supervisor Name] continued to make inappropriate comments and gestures toward [Client Name]. This included telling her, "I want to do so much for you, but now I can't because of this situation." This retaliatory remark was intended to condemn [Client Name] for reporting [Supervisor Name]'s illegal conduct, implying that she has damaged her own career by doing so.

Subsequent to [Client Name]'s refusal to sign the [Date] memo, [Defendant Company Name] management prepared a second memo on [Date].

While this memo appears to acknowledge that [Supervisor Name] had engaged in some wrongful conduct, which [Defendant Company Name] alleges to have addressed, the memo also implies that [Client Name] was partially to blame for the situation exclusively created and controlled by [Supervisor Name]. As a result, [Client Name] again refused to sign this memo, which was especially offensive in light of her previous conversation with you about the October 16 memo.

CHAPTER 3

Demand

On [Date], [Client Name] was assigned to travel with [Supervisor Name] to a conference in [City, State]. She specifically requested that she and [Supervisor Name] travel separately, and that they have hotel rooms on separate floors. On the first night of their trip, [Supervisor Name] knocked on the door of [Client Name]'s room. He stated that his room was across the hall, and that his key did not work. He requested to enter [Client Name]'s room. [Client Name] refused to open the door, and stated she would call the front desk to obtain another key. [Client Name] was so upset by [Supervisor Name]'s transparent attempt to visit her room that she did not sleep all night.

On [Date], [Client Name] submitted written notice that she was leaving the company, effective [Date]. She could no longer work under the hostile, threatening, and intimidating circumstances caused by [Supervisor Name], which included requirements of traveling alone with him. Moreover, it had become clear to her that [Defendant Company Name] was either unwilling or unable to control and remedy [Supervisor Name]'s continuing illegal behavior. The events of the previous weeks, as well as [Supervisor Name]'s history of insensitivity to sexually inappropriate conduct, demonstrated that [Defendant Company Name] management was not responsive to her situation or her concerns, and had created an impossible work situation for her.

For the next 10 days, [Client Name] continued to attempt to perform her job responsibilities, notwithstanding her fear of communicating with [Supervisor Name]. During this time, [Client Name] learned that [Defendant Company Name] management had not informed [Supervisor Name] of her resignation. When she addressed this issue with you, you offered her no support or assistance and, astonishingly, instructed her to discuss the reasons for her resignation directly with [Supervisor Name]. On [Date], [Client Name] submitted a memo resigning, effective immediately.

The handling of this entire matter by [Defendant Company Name] management was highly improper, causing extreme anxiety and distress to [Client Name]. During [Client Name]'s employment, [Defendant Company

Name] exhibited offensive and illegal behavior, failed to properly investigate and remedy [Supervisor Name]'s outrageous conduct, retaliated against [Client Name] for complaining to corporate management, and knowingly continued to expose her to [Supervisor Name]'s harassment. These events, while actionable standing alone, are underscored by an apparently pervasive attitude of insensitivity by [Defendant Company Name] management regarding sexually offensive conduct in the work environment, including at least one recent example of giving an employee a farewell party at which the company served a cake with breasts on it.

Claims Against [Defendant Company Name]

As a result of [Supervisor Name]'s wrongful and illegal conduct in subjecting [Client Name] to extensive and repeated sexual harassment, failing to take appropriate corrective measures when notified of the discriminatory conduct, retaliating against her for reporting [Supervisor Name]'s conduct, and constructively discharging her by continuing to impose intolerable working conditions, [Client Name] has been damaged substantially. These damages include suffering financial losses, loss of employment benefits, damage to her career and professional reputation, and severe emotional distress from the degrading conduct and the ultimate loss of her job, to which she was deeply committed prior to the above events. [Client Name] has requested that we commence legal action on her behalf to seek redress for [Supervisor Name]'s illegal conduct, as outlined above.

I am writing at this time to afford [Defendant Company Name] an opportunity to review this matter, and to attempt a resolution without resort to protracted formal litigation. Accordingly, [Client Name] would be willing to resolve this matter, and release [Defendant Company Name] from further liability, by way of a settlement in the amount of $200,000. This amount is substantially less than recent Massachusetts court and agency awards against employers involving similar or less egregious conduct. It also represents appropriate compensation for the damage to [Client Name]'s career and reputation, as well as the severe emotional distress that she has suffered as a result of [Supervisor Name]'s illegal conduct.

Please contact me by [Date] to advise me of your position on this matter. If I do not hear from you by that date, I will pursue appropriate legal action on [Client Name]'s behalf.

The forgoing representations are for purposes of settlement discussions only, and are made under reservation of all rights and remedies. If you have any questions, please do not hesitate to contact me.

                    Sincerely,

                    Law Firm

                    Lawyer Name

cc: Client

CHAPTER 3

LETTERS FOR LITIGATORS

7. Demand Letter – Personal Injury

Date

Claims Adjuster
AAA Insurance Co.

RE: Claimants: Richard Smith and Joyce Jones
Your Insured: Megacompany, Inc./Davidson
Date of Incident: May 13, 2003
C.U. Claim No.: OB10377OQ

Dear Mr. Adjuster:

As you know from our recent telephone conversation, this Law Firm represents Richard Smith and Joyce Jones in connection with personal injuries they sustained on [Date], in an automobile collision with your insured, David Davidson, an agent or employee of Megacompany, Inc., in Anytown, Massachusetts. I am writing at this time to advise you in more detail of the nature of Mr. Smith's and Ms. Jones's claims, and the damages they have sustained as a result.

NATURE OF INCIDENT

On [Date], at approximately [Time], Mr. Smith and Ms. Jones were traveling in Mr. Smith's Ford Bronco automobile on Main Street in Anytown, Massachusetts. The weather was clear and dry. Mr. Smith put on his left turn signal, and then stopped on Main Street to make a left turn onto Short Street. At that time, Mr. Smith's vehicle was rear-ended at high speed by an 18-wheel truck driven by Mr. Davidson and registered to Megacompany, Inc. According to the police report (see Exhibit 1 attached hereto) and witness accounts, Mr. Davidson failed to stop, and plowed into the back of Mr. Smith's vehicle while traveling at excessive speed. The truck left approximately sixty (60) feet of skid marks on the road prior to impacting Mr. Smith's vehicle (see photographs attached as Exhibit 2).

As a result of this collision, Mr. Smith and Ms. Jones sustained severe personal injuries. They were both wearing seat belts, but were dislodged from the seat belts by the force of the impact. Mr. Smith was thrown against the steering wheel and was pinned between the steering wheel and the driver's door. Ms. Jones was thrown out of her seat belt and against the dashboard and the passenger door. They each briefly lost consciousness as a result of the impact.

CHAPTER 3

Demand

Mr. Smith telephoned 911 from his car phone, and the police, firefighters and ambulance arrived shortly thereafter. Medical personnel placed a collar on Ms. Jones's neck and inserted a backboard behind her. They then removed her on a stretcher and transported her by ambulance to Memorial Hospital, where she was treated for her injuries (see Exhibit 3). Mr. Davidson was issued a citation by the Anytown Police for speeding (see Exhibit 1).

Mr. Smith's car was also totaled (see photographs attached as Exhibit 4). His car was towed from the scene.

LIABILITY

Because of the nature of the incident involving a rear-end collision where my clients were lawfully stopped, which is confirmed by the police report, liability on the part of your insured appears to be clear. If you dispute the liability of your insured or have any information to the contrary, please advise me immediately in writing so we may further discuss this issue.

INJURIES SUSTAINED BY MS. JONES

This collision caused Ms. Jones, who is 50 years old, to sustain severe personal injuries. Medical reports indicate that she had a brief loss of consciousness at the time of the accident. She has also suffered, and continues to suffer from, pain in her back, neck, shoulders and arm, all of which have persisted since this incident. In addition, Ms. Jones suffered bruises to her head, face, both of her legs and her arms. These injuries, and the medical treatment received by Ms. Jones, are detailed in the medical reports of Marcus Welby, M.D., attached as Exhibit 5, and are summarized as follows:

1. Back Injuries—Ms. Jones suffered a severe myofascial injury to her cervical spine. She has experienced persistent pain, a limited range of motion, and continues to suffer pain and tightness in the back, as well as limitations in her ability to stand or sit for prolonged periods, and to bend or lift. She also remains unable to drive a car for any extended period of time without experiencing pain. These injuries are further detailed in the medical reports of Dr. Welby (Exhibit 5). She was prescribed a back brace, which she must continue to use regularly for support and pain relief. As noted in Dr. Welby's report, she will likely have permanent impairment of 20 percent in her back, and her condition will probably worsen over time.

2. Neck Injuries—Ms. Jones also suffered injuries to her neck that have caused her persistent pain and a limited range of motion (see medical

reports of Dr. Welby). As a result of these injuries, she was placed by her treating physician in a neck collar for several weeks after this incident. To date, she continues to suffer from chronic pain and limited mobility in her neck.

3. Shoulder Injuries—Ms. Jones was diagnosed by Dr. Welby with a possible rotator cuff tear on her right side. She had very limited mobility and severe pain in her right shoulder, which continues to the present.

4. Other Injuries—In addition to the foregoing, the impact of this accident caused Ms. Jones to suffer from lacerations, abrasions, and bruises to her head, face, arms and legs (see photographs attached as Exhibit 6). The contusion to her right forearm was especially severe, causing her severe pain and limitations at work. For several months following the accident, Ms. Jones also suffered from persistent and severe headaches, nausea and a loss of sleep. This interfered with her job performance, as well as her household and leisure activities.

In addition, Ms. Jones was given a Cortisone injection for pain relief. She suffered a severe allergic reaction to this injection and was rushed to the hospital in extreme pain. She was unable to move and vomited in the doctor's office. She was placed on alternate medication as a result of this reaction.

Finally, the stress from this incident caused an aggravation of Ms. Jones's ulcer, which had previously been unremarkable. She was in severe gastrointestinal pain for several months, and had to resume a regime of medical treatment and prescription medication to control this condition.

As a result of the foregoing injuries, Ms. Jones was forced to undergo extensive medical treatment, including regular physical therapy and ulcer treatment, which is detailed in Exhibit 7.

INJURIES SUSTAINED BY MR. SMITH

Mr. Smith, who is 54 years old, similarly suffered severe injuries as a result of this collision. The impact caused him to lose consciousness as he was crushed between the seat and the steering wheel. He suffered from dizziness and a concussion for several days following the accident. Mr. Smith suffered injuries to his neck, back, head, arms and legs, which have caused him great pain and mobility limitations for the past year. These injuries, and the medical treatment received by Mr. Smith, are detailed in the medical reports of Dr. Welby and Dr. Green, attached as Exhibits 8 and 9. A summary of Mr. Smith's injuries is as follows:

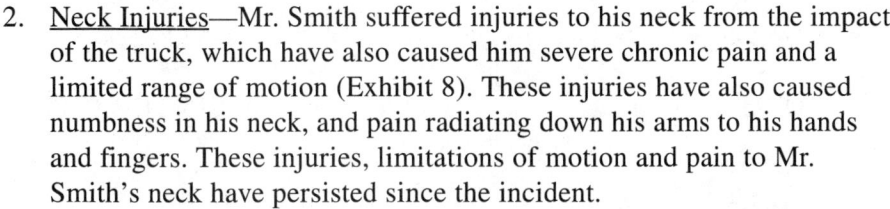

CHAPTER 3

Demand

1. Back Injuries—Mr. Smith suffered a severe myofascial injury of his cervical and lumbar spine. These injuries have caused, and continue to cause, severe pain, a limited range of motion, and tightness in his back, as well as limitations in his ability to stand or sit or drive a car for prolonged periods. He cannot freely bend down or lift heavy objects. This has substantially impaired his work as a firefighter, as well as numerous other activities. These injuries are further detailed in the medical reports of Dr. Welby (attached as Exhibit 8). As noted in Dr. Welby's report, Mr. Smith has also suffered permanent impairment of 25 to 35 percent in his back and neck, which has severely impacted his work as a firefighter.

2. Neck Injuries—Mr. Smith suffered injuries to his neck from the impact of the truck, which have also caused him severe chronic pain and a limited range of motion (Exhibit 8). These injuries have also caused numbness in his neck, and pain radiating down his arms to his hands and fingers. These injuries, limitations of motion and pain to Mr. Smith's neck have persisted since the incident.

3. Headaches—Mr. Smith was initially diagnosed by Dr. Welby with severe post-concussional headaches. These severe headaches have continued to cause Mr. Smith pain, discomfort, and interference with his daily activities since the incident, and continue to the present.

4. Other Injuries—In addition to the above injuries, the impact of this accident caused Mr. Smith to suffer from multiple lacerations, contusions, abrasions, and bruises to his head, face, arms and legs, causing him severe pain. For several months following the accident, Mr. Smith also suffered from persistent and severe headaches, nausea and a loss of sleep. This interfered with his job performance and leisure activities.

Furthermore, the stress of this incident and its impact on Mr. Smith's job as a firefighter has caused an exacerbation of his high blood pressure, requiring medication to keep this condition under control.

MEDICAL AND OTHER ITEMIZED EXPENSES
As a result of the above, Ms. Jones and Mr. Smith have each incurred substantial medical expenses and other damages, which are itemized as follows:

A. Joyce Jones

1. Medical and Hospital Expenses (Exhibit 10)	$8,838.37
2. Prescription Medication (Exhibit 11)	$ 273.09
TOTAL	$9,111.46

B. Richard Smith

1. Medical Expenses (Exhibit 12)	$5,191.99
2. Prescription Medication (Exhibit 13)	$ 56.00
3. Towing (Exhibit 14)	$ 45.00
4. Automobile Rental (Exhibit 15)	$ 176.64
5. Automobile Damage (Exhibit 16)	$7,822.50
TOTAL	$13,292.13

LOST WAGES

A. Joyce Jones

As a result of the above-described injuries, Ms. Jones was unable to return to her employment as an Office Manager with the Little Company for a period of two weeks. Thereafter, she was absent for an additional two-week period, and was then caused to lose time from work periodically due to continuing pain and to obtain medical treatment. Her total lost time from work was nine weeks.

At the time of the incident, Ms. Jones's salary was $46,575 per year. In addition, she received full health insurance, paid vacations, legal holidays and sick pay, accumulated on a per diem basis for days worked. Accordingly, Ms. Jones has lost a total of $8,061 in wages, plus the loss of accrued benefits.

B. Richard Smith

Mr. Smith also lost a significant amount of time from work as a firefighter for the City of Anytown as a result of your insured's negligence. He was totally disabled from work for a period of eight weeks. Thereafter, he was partially disabled for several days over the next few months, and was caused to lose an additional five days from work due to continuing pain and to obtain medical treatment. Accordingly, his total lost time from work was nine weeks.

At the time of the incident, Mr. Smith's salary was $34,000 per year, plus approximately $3,500 in incentive pay for nights, weekends, arson squad work and other elevated duties that he regularly assumed. In addition, he received full health insurance, paid vacations, legal holidays and sick pay, accumulated on a per diem basis for days worked. Accordingly, Mr. Smith has lost a total of $6,490.38 in wages, plus the loss of accrued benefits. Moreover, he is likely to have future restrictions on his ability to take on elevated duties, which have historically increased his wages by approximately $3,000 to $4,000 per year.

PAIN AND SUFFERING

In addition to the damages referenced above, Ms. Jones and Mr. Smith have each incurred extreme pain and suffering, impairment of their daily activities, and loss of enjoyment of physical and recreational activities. Prior to the accident, Ms. Jones's activities included regular exercise, walking, and recreational activities with her grandson. She also took care of her home, including interior and exterior maintenance. Since this incident, Ms. Jones's ability to get around has become much more limited, and physical exertion in any respect has become nearly impossible.

Prior to this incident, Ms. Jones was also enrolled in classes at State University, working toward her Bachelor of Science degree. She was scheduled to graduate in [Month, Year]. Because of the pain caused by the collision, Ms. Jones was unable to sit through her classes. As a result, she had to withdraw from her program (see Exhibit 17) and has been unable to complete her degree. This has caused her great anxiety and depression, as she was very dedicated to completing her degree, and has now had an extended period of time away from her classes.

Finally, as a result of the pain she has suffered, Ms. Jones has been required to take both prescription and over-the-counter medication. These medications have caused her side effects, such as grogginess, upset stomach, and anxiety. The above-referenced pain and physical limitations that Ms. Jones has suffered have also caused her emotional stress, exacerbation of her ulcer, and depression.

Similarly, Mr. Smith has suffered from a loss of enjoyment and impairment of his leisure, family, household, and recreational activities. These included weight training, regular exercise, running, ice hockey, and recreational activities with his grandchildren, all of which have been severely restricted since the incident. He has been severely depressed over the impact of this incident on his ability to fully perform his job as a firefighter, which he has done without restriction for over 29 years. Mr. Smith has also had to take a variety of prescription and non-prescription medications for his pain and inability to sleep. All of the above have caused him extreme emotional distress and anxiety, as his life has been altered substantially from this motor vehicle accident.

SUMMARY OF SPECIAL DAMAGES

A. Joyce Jones

Medical $9,111.46
Lost Wages $8,061.00

TOTAL $17,172.46

B. Richard Smith

Medical $5,247.99
Lost Wages .... $6,490.38 (plus loss of future earnings)

Automobile Damage ... $8,044.14

TOTAL $19,782.51

DEMAND

As the foregoing information indicates, Ms. Jones's and Mr. Smith's lives have been altered irreparably as a result of your insured's negligence. Recent jury verdicts in Suffolk County in cases of this nature have resulted in awards well in excess of $150,000 per claimant. It is my hope, however, that we can resolve this claim expeditiously and without resort to formal litigation.

Accordingly, Ms. Jones and Mr. Smith would each be willing to settle this matter short of litigation in the amount of $90,000 per claimant. If these amounts are in excess of the limits of your insured's coverage, demand is hereby made for immediate payment of the policy limits so my clients may bring any appropriate claims pursuant to the underinsurance provisions of their own automobile policies, or directly against the responsible parties.

Please contact me by not later than [Date] to advise me of your position on this matter. In the meantime, if you have any questions, or if I may provide any additional information, please do not hesitate to contact me.

CHAPTER 3

Demand

                Sincerely,

                Law Firm

                Lawyer Name

Enclosures
cc: Client

8. Demand Letter – Personal Injury – Alternate

Date

VIA CERTIFIED MAIL NO. XXXXXXXXX
RETURN RECEIPT REQUESTED

Name
Company Name
Address 1
Address 2
City, State, Zip Code

Re:

Dear _____:

This letter serves as a demand for settlement in the above-referenced matter and provides you with the relevant background to support the settlement demand. I have enclosed documents including a police accident report, medical chronology, certified medical records and medical bills, employer's lost wages statement, and photographs of the accident scene and bodily injuries. These documents substantiate [Client Name]'s claim that he suffered severe injuries to his abdomen, neck, back, left arm, shin and hip as a result of an automobile accident caused by your insured, [Name]. This letter is for settlement purposes only, and in no way do any of the representations in this letter serve as an admission of any liability or a waiver of any claims or defenses on the part of [Client Name].

FACTS

On [Date], [Client Name], then a [___]-year-old male, was the owner and operator of a [Year Make Auto]. [Client Name] was driving [describe scenario and location]. Your insured, [Name], was driving [describe scenario and location]. [Name] (describe what insured did to cause accident), causing a collision. [Name] was cited for "Failure to Grant Right of Way to Other Vehicle." (See enclosed photos of venue and Police Report.) Upon impact, [Client Name] (describe what physically happened to your client as a result of impact).

INJURIES

[Ambulance Name] was called to transport [Client Name] to the [Hospital Name]. When the ambulance attendants arrived on the accident scene, they found [Client Name] (e.g., lying supine on the street in extreme pain). He had [detail injuries found by EMTs]. He was (e.g., immobilized on a longboard and head pads, given an IV and oxygen), and was transported to the [Hospital Name] Emergency Room where he was met by the trauma team.

Demand

At [Hospital Name] [Client Name] complained of [describe hospital records] (e.g., severe left-sided chest pain, abdominal pain with nausea and vomiting, abrasions to his chest, left hip and left knee). A series of x-rays and CAT scans of the abdomen were ordered. The CAT scan revealed a large amount of free blood and fluid in his abdomen. An emergency laparotomy was ordered to explore [Client Name]'s abdomen for a suspected ruptured bowel. He went directly to the operating room, where he underwent a *two-hour surgery* that was performed by [Doctor Name]. The exploratory surgery resulted in a *surgical resection of his small bowel*, which had *three (3) areas of perforation*. There was *significant bruising and multiple mesenteric rents* scattered throughout the jejunum through to the ileum. The rents were repaired with sutures and the multiple bleeding points were secured with suture ligatures. His operative incision was *full-length midline*, necessitating a staple closure. After surgery, he was admitted to the Intensive Care Unit, where he remained for five (5) days.

During his hospital course, [Client Name]'s pain was severe and persistent (e.g., necessitating the use of a patient-controlled morphine administration device). He suffered choking discomfort from nasal-gastric tubing, and was placed in wrist restraints. Frequent suction was necessary for copious nasal secretions. His abdomen was tender, especially at the incision site. At times he was extremely uncomfortable due to skin itching and hypersensitivity of his extremities. He underwent daily chest x-rays, blood tests, and dressing changes. The abrasions to his back, arm and leg were extensive and required open-air healing. He was unable to eat or drink for 5 days, resulting in a high nutrition deficit risk. Despite these injuries, [Client Name] was proactive in his healing process, and was released from the ICU on [Date]. He was discharged from the [Hospital Name] to his wife's care on [Date]. He was given a prescription for Percocet for pain control after discharge.

At his initial post-op checkup on [Date], [Doctor Name] noted that [Client Name] was complaining of abdominal pain. [Doctor Name] had an extensive discussion with [Client Name] regarding *restrictions of his physical activities* during the healing process. The abdominal staples were removed at this time.

On [Date], [Client Name] consulted with [Name], a neurologist. Upon examination of [Client Name], [Doctor Name] noted a "diminished range

CHAPTER 3

LETTERS FOR LITIGATORS

of movement over the cervical greater than lumber spine with muscle spasm palpated diffusely in the paravertebral regions localized." [Doctor Name] recommended that [Client Name] undergo physical therapy.

At [Client Name]'s initial visit with [Doctor Name] on [Date], the doctor's impression was of "cervical and lumbar strains." [Doctor Name] also recommended a physical therapy program. [Client Name] began a physical therapy program with [Clinic Name]. [Client Name] cooperated with his physical therapist's treatment plan, but found that the therapy was too painful because of his internal injuries, so he discontinued further treatment.

MEDICAL EXPENSES INCURRED TO DATE
(See Detailed Medical Chronology)

Ambulance	$
Hospital	$
Pharmacy	$
Physician	$
Physician	$
Physician	$
Physical Therapist	$
Other	$
Total Medical Expenses to Date:	$

LOST WAGES

At the time of his accident, [Client Name] was employed at [Employer Name] as a [Position]. He was placed on medical leave from the date of the accident, [Date], until [Date], a total of XXX weeks. His missed wages totaled [$_____]. This does not include the potential additional money he could have made from overtime hours.

CONCLUSION

As a direct and proximate result of his automobile/motorcycle accident, [Client Name] was totally disabled and unable to work for ____ weeks. He underwent a two-hour emergency surgery immediately following the accident and seven days' hospitalization, including five days of intensive care. In addition, he undertook a strenuous physical therapy program that caused more pain than relief. [Client Name]'s surgical scar is substantial (11 inches) and permanent (see photos of scar enclosed), and his pain and immobility continues, including numbness and stiffness across his shoulders, neck, and back. [Client Name] was a dedicated bodybuilder, but can no longer perform the exercises and weight-lifting routines that he enjoyed prior to the accident. His ability to enjoy sexual relations is diminished due to his decreased abdominal strength and his embarrassment regarding his scar. In addition, [Client Name] experiences ongoing emotional distress from the trauma of the accident and his resultant injuries.

Liability is not an issue as [Client Name] was in no way responsible for the accident and his resulting injuries. As noted in the police report, the investigating [City Name] patrolman stated that [Insured Name] "failed to grant right of way to other vehicle." Therefore, demand for settlement is made at this time in the amount of [$_____].

Demand

Sincerely,

Law Firm

Lawyer Name

Enclosures
cc: Client (with enclosures)

CHAPTER 3

LETTERS FOR LITIGATORS

9. Demand Letter – Personal Injury – Post-Suit

Date

Name
Company Name
Address 1
Address 2
City, State, Zip Code

Re:

Dear _____:

In follow-up to our conversation yesterday, this letter sets forth Mr. White's settlement demand in this matter. All statements herein are made for settlement purposes only and are made without prejudice.

It is highly likely, if not certain, that there will be a liability finding, either by the court on summary judgment or by a jury, in favor of Mr. White. The police report and Mr. White both indicate that defendant Smith failed to stop at the stop sign at Quarantine Road and I-695 while within the scope of his employment with you and struck the right rear of the vehicle Mr. White was driving. It is also possible that a default judgment will be entered against Mr. Smith, as he has not answered the complaint, nor has an attorney entered an appearance on his behalf.

According to Dr. Marlene Jones's report of March 15, 2003, the motor vehicle collision not only caused permanent injury to his bones, joints, ligaments, ligamentum flavum, annular fibers and joint capsules but also dramatically increased Mr. White's facet arthritis and foraminal stenosis. She believes he will have continued pain on a daily basis that will need to be medically managed with physical therapy, injections, and pain medication.

Mr. White's injuries have been and continue to be serious, painful, and disabling. He was unable to work from 05-12-02 through 07-31-02 due to stiffness in the neck and pain in the lower back and incurred lost wages of at least $8,500. He has medical bills that exceed $5,000.

It is quite likely that the fact-finder will award significant damages for pain and suffering, especially in view of the fact that this is a permanent injury that Dr. Jones states will worsen over time. Mr. White has authorized me to make a demand to settle this claim in the amount of $85,000. I would appreciate hearing your thoughts regarding settlement.

Sincerely,

Law Firm

Lawyer Name

10. Demand Letter – Notice to Quit

Date

VIA CERTIFIED MAIL AND FIRST CLASS MAIL

Name
Company Name
Address 1
Address 2
City, State, Zip Code

Re:

Dear _____:

You are hereby notified to quit and deliver up in 14 days from the date hereof the premises that you hold as a tenant of _____, namely _____.

You have a right to prevent termination of your tenancy by paying or tendering to your landlord, your landlord's attorney, or the person to whom you customarily pay your rent the full amount of rent due within ten days after receipt of this notice.

If you have any questions, please do not hesitate to contact me.

Sincerely,

Law Firm

Lawyer Name

11. Demand Letter – Administrative Tribunal

Date

Name
Company Name
Address 1
Address 2
City, State, Zip Code

Re:

Dear _____:

I am writing to you in the hope that the parties will be able to resolve this matter without the need for a hearing before the Board. Accordingly, this letter is submitted for purposes of settlement and without prejudice to the rights of ABC Industries, Inc. ("ABC").

As demonstrated by the materials submitted by ABC under Board Rule 4, ABC incurred $6,206.61 in out-of-pocket costs to outside vendors and $14,142.99 in labor costs in performing this project, for a total of $20,349.60. See materials attached at tabs 2 and 3 of ABC's submission. These costs do not include certain other direct costs that cannot be determined with exactitude, such as fuel costs, nor, more significantly, do they include any allowance for the use of and wear and tear on ABC's equipment. As you are aware, the state has paid and contends that it was only obligated to pay $5,418.87 for ABC's services.

As admitted by the state agency, ABC submitted bids for this contract on the basis of representations that the weight of the material to be removed would be "approximately sixty (60) tons" and that this weight had been "estimated" in a manner that would produce "a reasonable weight." See Complaint and Answer at paragraphs 2,3.

The Board has held that a contractor has a right to rely upon estimates stated by state agencies in preparing its bid. See Appeal of Martin G. Imbach, Inc. (MSBCA Docket No. MDOT 1020) (1983) (MICPEL compilation ¶ 52); Appeal of Hardaway Constructors, Inc. (MSBCA Docket No. 1249) (1989) (MICPEL compilation ¶ 227). As a U.S. court of claims case quoted by the Board in the latter opinion states, "Assuming that the bidder acts reasonably, he is entitled to rely on Government estimates as repre-

CHAPTER 3

LETTERS FOR LITIGATORS

senting honest and informed conclusions." *Weeks Dredging & Contracting, Inc. v. United States,* 13 Cl. Ct. 1983 (1987) at 228, 235, quoted in the *Hardaway Constructors, Inc.* opinion at 41.

Moreover, the contract documents do not merely estimate the weight of the material at 60 tons but describe the scope of work as the removal of "approximately" 60 tons. The words "approximate" and "approximately" when used in contract documents have been consistently construed by the courts as meaning nearly correct or exact so as not to permit substantial deviation. In this regard, I am enclosing for your review copies of the opinions rendered in the cases of *Eastern Service Management Company v. United States,* 363 F.2d 729 (4th Cir. 1966) (cleaning contractor held entitled to additional compensation where space to be cleaned was 8,700 square feet larger then "approximately 129,300 square feet" represented by government in contract); *Urban Masonry Corporation v. N&N Contractors, Inc.*, 676 A.2d 26 (D.C. App. 1996) (contract obligating contractor to install "approx. 297 (+/–) panels" did not obligate it to install an additional 68 panels); *Johnsrud v. Lind,* 219 N.W.2d 181 (N.D. 1974) (seller who was obligated to deliver "approximately" 600 steers and 300 heifers did not comply with contract by delivering 398 steers and 341 heifers); *Smith v. Osborn,* 223 N.W. 2d 913 (Wis. 1974) (contract calling for sale of "approximately 70 acres" of land was not satisfied by delivery of 53.59 acres). Obviously, a contract calling for the removal of "approximately 60 tons" of material, with the contractor to be paid by the ton, is not fulfilled where the contractor is only afforded the removal of 9.85 tons.

As indicated in the complaint, ABC is willing to reduce the gross compensation payable to it from $33,008.40 to $32,000 in view of the cost savings realized by not having to pay dump fees on 50.15 tons of material at $20 per ton. (The actual invoice for the dump fees submitted by Atlantic Waste Reduction is included in the material under tab 1 of ABC's submission.) After crediting the state's payment of $5,418.87, ABC is, therefore, justly due $26,581.13 plus interest. However, in the interest of a prompt settlement of this matter, **ABC would be willing to accept the sum of Twenty-Five Thousand Dollars ($25,000.00)** in full settlement of this claim. However, this amount would have to be paid prior to the time when ABC must begin formal preparation for the hearing scheduled for March 21, 2004. If this matter is not resolved and the settlement payment received by no later than March 7, 2004, this offer shall be deemed withdrawn. Accordingly, please contact me regarding this proposal as soon as possible.

We respectfully submit that in view of the facts of this matter and the applicable legal authorities, the state's continued refusal to make a fair settlement of this claim could be construed as lacking in good faith or substantial justification so as to warrant the award to ABC of its attorney's fees and other litigation costs pursuant to § 15-221.2 of State Finance and Procurement Article. ABC reserves this remedy, as well as all of its other rights and remedies.

Sincerely,

Law Firm

Lawyer Name

B. Response

1. Response – Employment

Date

Name
Company Name
Address 1
Address 2
City, State, Zip Code

    Re:

Dear _____:

This Law Firm has been retained by _____ in connection with matters pertaining to your client _____. Your Chapter 93A demand letter dated _____ to _____ has been referred to me for a response.

Your letter raises numerous allegations arising during the period of _____'s employment with _____, as well as additional allegations arising under a _____ Agreement between your client and _____ subsequent to his employment. While the factual and legal basis for many of these allegations is unclear from your letter, I will attempt to respond to them, and will hope that we can have the opportunity to discuss and clarify some of these issues.

As a threshold matter, and as I am sure you are aware, disputes between employers and employees concerning the terms and conditions of employment are exempt from the provisions of G.L. c. 93A. <u>Falmouth OB-GYN Associates, Inc. v. Abisla</u>, 417 Mass. 176 (1994); <u>Anzalone v. M.B.T.A.</u>, 403 Mass. 119, 122 (1988); <u>Manning v. Zuckerman</u>, 388 Mass. 8, 10-15 (1983). Moreover, to the extent your client's claims concern stock ownership issues, such claims are also exempt from the scope of Chapter 93A. <u>Puritan Medical Center, Inc. v. Cashman</u>, 413 Mass. 167, 180 (1992); <u>Zimmerman v. Bogoff</u>, 402 Mass. 650 (1988); <u>Riseman v. Orion Research, Inc.</u>, 394 Mass. 311, 313-314 (1985).

Furthermore, to the extent your client's claims arise out of the Marketing Agent Agreement, those claims are subject to the arbitration provisions contained in Paragraph 12 of that Agreement, and the Limitations of Liability provisions of Paragraph 13 of that Agreement. Therefore, filing a civil lawsuit against _____ at this stage is prohibited, and would subject both you and your client to court sanctions and attorney's fees for the filing of a frivolous suit, which is expressly barred by the agreement between these parties.

Notwithstanding the above procedural and jurisdictional deficiencies in your demand letter, please be advised that _____ expressly denies the substantive allegations contained in your letter, and specifically denies that it has engaged in any unfair and deceptive acts or practices. Even assuming the truth of the allegations in your letter, which _____ denies, these claims amount to mere employment or contractual disputes, which do not in themselves constitute a violation of G.L.c. 93A. <u>Atkinson v. Rosenthal</u>, 33 Mass. App. Ct. 219 (1992); <u>Canal Elec. Co. v. Westinghouse Electric Corp.</u>, 756 F. Supp. 620, 628 (D. Mass. 1990).

Your client was employed by, and under contract with, _____ for a relatively brief period of time. During this relationship, your client failed to meet his employment and contractual obligations to _____ in numerous respects. During the period of his Marketing Agent Agreement, he failed to make a single sale. In summary, your client's conduct includes, but is not limited to, failing to provide services to _____ as required by his employment and his contract, communicating with third parties in a manner that was knowingly detrimental to _____'s business interests, and violating the confidentiality and noncompetition provisions of his contract with _____. As a result, _____ lawfully terminated its relationship with your client, and is not liable to _____ for any damages or other compensation whatsoever.

Finally, it has come to the attention of _____ that, both during and subsequent to your client's relationship with _____, he has committed numerous violations of the Nondisclosure, Noncompetition and Developments Agreement he executed with _____. _____'s violations of this agreement have caused _____ significant damages, and will entitle _____ to monetary and injunctive relief should this matter proceed to litigation. Your client has also unlawfully retained certain materials and other property belonging to _____ in violation of the agreements between these parties and applicable law.

Please be advised that if your client institutes any claim against _____, such claims will be vigorously defended, and _____ will assert counterclaims for damages caused by _____'s conduct; will seek immediate injunctive relief to enjoin your

CHAPTER 3

Demand

client from further violations of the Nondisclosure, Noncompetition and Developments Agreement; and will seek costs, attorney's fees, and sanctions for the institution of frivolous litigation.

If you have any questions, please do not hesitate to contact me.

Sincerely,

Law Firm

Lawyer Name

CHAPTER 4

Mediation/Arbitration

Mediation and arbitration present additional opportunities to resolve disputes. Arbitration mirrors litigation, and for the most part, letters used in the context of litigation apply equally well to arbitration.

Mediation, on the other hand, focuses on bringing the parties to agreement voluntarily through techniques employed by a trained, neutral third party and, for this reason, is less adversarial than litigation or arbitration. If your goal is to resolve the dispute through mediation, the use of an upbeat and conciliatory style in your letters and your word choice can help set the stage.

A. To Opposing Counsel

1. Mediation – Scheduling

Date

Name
Company Name
Address 1
Address 2
City, State, Zip Code

Re:

Dear _____:

In response to your fax of yesterday, my letter to you of [Date] of last year stated that plaintiffs are amenable to mediating this matter prior to undertaking additional discovery. We have been waiting since then to hear your position on the matter.

Now that you have the agreement of your client, I see no reason the mediation cannot be accomplished before month's end, and if the case is not settled at that time, we can proceed with discovery, which would include the deposition of your client, as already noticed, for [Date].

Because of the [Date] discovery deadline, we should coordinate our calendars immediately to schedule the mediation some time in the next few weeks.

Sincerely,

Law Firm

Lawyer Name

cc: Client

B. To the Client

1. Mediation – Scheduling

Mediation/Arbitration

Date

Name
Company Name
Address 1
Address 2
City, State, Zip Code

Re:

Dear _____:

Please allow this to confirm that the mediation has been scheduled for Wednesday, June 6, at 10:00 a.m. at the law offices of Brown and White, 7 E. Broad Street, Baltimore, MD 21202. The mediation could take all day, so please come prepared to stay all day, and do not make any other plans for later in the day. There will be periods of time when the defendant and his lawyer will be meeting alone with the judge and we will simply be sitting and waiting for our own turn to do the same. Feel free to dress comfortably, and bring any snacks, refreshments, or reading material you might want as well as any medication you may need to take during the day.

If you like, we can meet beforehand to discuss what we can expect at the mediation, although this is not necessary, as we will have plenty of time to confer privately during the mediation itself. Please let me know whether you would like to meet beforehand and, if so, whether you would like to do it the morning of the mediation or some other day.

Sincerely,

Law Firm

Lawyer Name

2. Mediation – Statement

Date

Name
Company Name
Address 1
Address 2
City, State, Zip Code

Re:

Dear _____:

Enclosed herewith please find mediation statement recently submitted to the mediator.

This will confirm that we are scheduled to meet in my office at the above address on Thursday, July 20, at 9 a.m. to prepare and we will proceed to the mediation from there.

Sincerely,

Law Firm

Lawyer Name

Enclosure

CHAPTER 5

Complaint/Answer

While electronic filing, with its instant documentation of the transaction, is now the norm in some jurisdictions, paper filing remains the status quo in others. Transmittal letters can be useful when filing a complaint, answer or other pleading in a non-e-filing district or when the particular filing is unusual, such as a sealed complaint. Even when the filing is plain vanilla, though, a transmittal letter to the court performs the valuable function of documenting the who, what, when, and where of the transaction for the client and the file.

Sometimes, for whatever reason, opposing counsel has not received copies of a complaint through normal channels and will ask you to supply it. This can be a good time to let him or her know about any discovery you served with the complaint so it does not fall through the cracks.

Lawyers routinely give each other informal extensions of time to meet various deadlines. The degree of formality varies with the lawyers' mutual trust. However, it is always a good practice to memorialize extensions of time to file an answer to the complaint in writing, since the court may grant a default judgment when a timely answer is not filed. A letter memorializing the extension can be a valuable tool in getting any such default vacated.

CHAPTER 5

LETTERS FOR LITIGATORS

A. To the Court

1. Court – Complaint

Date

Clerk of Court at Courthouse
Address 1
Address 2
City, State, Zip Code

Re:

Dear _____:

Enclosed herewith please find the original and one copy of a civil complaint and demand for jury trial and the civil non-domestic case information report together with a filing fee in the amount of [$_____] in the above-captioned matter.

Please file the original and return a date-stamped copy to the deliverer of this letter. Please forward the writ of summons to my offices for private process service.

Thank you for your time and assistance.

Sincerely,

Law Firm

Lawyer Name

Enclosure
cc: Client

2. Court – Sealed Complaint

Date

**CONFIDENTIAL—FALSE CLAIMS ACT
COMPLAINT TO BE FILED UNDER SEAL**

Clerk of Court at Courthouse
Address 1
Address 2
City, State, Zip Code

    Re:

Dear _____:

Please accept for filing an original and three copies of Plaintiff's civil False Claims Act Complaint and Demand for Jury Trial, Motion to File Complaint in Camera and Place Complaint Under Seal and Proposed Order, and Request to Withhold Issue of Summons.

Pursuant to 31 U.S. § 3730(b)(2), these papers are filed in Camera and under seal. Accordingly, please withhold issuance of summonses and ensure that no copies are placed in the press box and that the action is not noted on the PACER computer system or otherwise on the public docket.

Thank you for your time and assistance.

                      Sincerely,

                      Law Firm

                      Lawyer Name

Enclosures
cc: Client

3. Court – Answer

Date

Clerk of Court at Courthouse
Address 1
Address 2
City, State, Zip Code

Re:

Dear _____:

Enclosed herewith please find the original and one copy of Defendant [Client Name]'s Answer to Complaint and civil Non-Domestic Case Information Report in the above-referenced matter.

Please file the original and return a date-stamped copy to my offices via first class U.S. mail. I have enclosed a self-addressed stamped envelope for your convenience.

Thank you for your time and assistance.

Sincerely,

Law Firm

Lawyer Name

Enclosure

cc: Client
    Opposing Counsel

B. Opposing Counsel

1. Opposing Counsel – Extension of Time

Complaint/
Answer

Date

Name
Company Name
Address 1
Address 2
City, State, Zip Code

    Re:

Dear _____:

This letter will confirm our agreement that the time for [Name] to file a responsive pleading in the above matter has been extended up to and including [Date].

Thank you for your courtesy and cooperation in this matter.

                Sincerely,

                Law Firm

                Lawyer Name

CHAPTER 5
LETTERS FOR LITIGATORS

2. Opposing Counsel – Complaint

Date

Name
Company Name
Address 1
Address 2
City, State, Zip Code

Re:

Dear _____:

Pursuant to your request, enclosed are copies of the Complaint and Demand for Jury Trial with Exhibits together with Plaintiff's First Request for Production of Documents that were personally served on your client on [Date].

It has been over six weeks since your client was served with these pleadings and the responses are now overdue. Please let me know at your earliest convenience when you will be providing the responses.

Sincerely,

Law Firm

Lawyer Name

Enclosure

C. Client

1. Client – Draft Complaint

CHAPTER 5
Complaint/Answer

Date

Name
Company Name
Address 1
Address 2
City, State, Zip Code

Re:

Dear _____:

Following up on our discussions, enclosed for your careful review please find a draft of a proposed Complaint in this matter. Although I have tried to draft the Complaint from the information and documents you have provided, I must ultimately rely on your personal knowledge of these facts to make sure the Complaint is accurate and complete. This is an important legal document, and before it is filed we must try to make sure that there are no misstatements or exaggerations. With this in mind, please review it carefully and make any suggested corrections, changes, or additions either directly on this draft or in a separate memo directly from you to me (to preserve the attorney-client privilege), or both. Then return the document(s) to me as soon as possible so that I can continue to move forward on this matter.

As always, if you have any problems, comments, or questions, please let me know.

Sincerely,

Law Firm

Lawyer Name

Enclosure

2. Client – Answer and Scheduling Letter

Date

Name
Company Name
Address 1
Address 2
City, State, Zip Code

Re:

Dear _____:

Please allow this to serve as a status report. The defendants filed an answer to our complaint; please find a copy enclosed for your records.

I have also enclosed a pre-trial scheduling order regarding your case. Please mark your calendars; your attendance is mandatory at the pre-trial conference of [Date], and at the trial beginning on [Date].

Be aware, however, that the trial date is subject to change, and the trial itself may not start until a few days to weeks later depending on the condition of the court's trial calendar at that time. The trial may take as long as several days. It may be possible to settle the case before trial, but for planning purposes we must assume the case will go forward.

Please feel free to contact me if you have any questions or comments.

Sincerely,

Law Firm

Lawyer Name

Enclosure

3. Client – Forwarding Complaint – Insurer's Counsel

Complaint/Answer

Date

PERSONAL AND CONFIDENTIAL

Name
Company Name
Address 1
Address 2
City, State, Zip Code

Re:

Dear _____:

As you know, [Firm Name] has been appointed to represent you in the above matter by [Insurance Company Client].

As we discussed on the telephone, we have entered our appearance on your behalf (a copy of which is enclosed), and we are required to enter an answer to the plaintiff's complaint with the Court by [Date]. I would like to meet with you at your earliest convenience to discuss plaintiff's allegations, and to investigate the events surrounding his claims. Please call our office upon receipt of this letter to arrange for a time and place to meet with me.

We look forward to working with you.

Sincerely,

Law Firm

Lawyer Name

Enclosure

cc: Client Insurance Company Claim Rep.

CHAPTER 6

Written Discovery Letters

Discovery is at the heart of all litigation, and written discovery creates the foundation for everything else that follows—depositions and other examinations, and eventually motions and trial.

Often the opposition forgets or refuses to respond to discovery, or responds inadequately. Bringing these issues to opposing counsel's attention in a letter not only serves as a request to rectify the problem, but it also creates a paper trail that can be used as an exhibit to a motion to compel, should that be necessary down the road.

Few things are more convincing to a judge contemplating a motion to compel than a sheaf of polite letters from you, which opposing counsel ignored, requesting responses or supplemental responses to discovery. Many jurisdictions require such letters, sometimes known as "good faith" letters, as a precondition to filing a motion to compel.

Negotiations between counsel regarding resolution of discovery disputes, the timing of discovery, and supplementation of previous responses should all be memorialized in letters so the file is documented. When copied to the client, these letters also serve as a status report to keep the client informed and aware that you are at work on his or her behalf.

CHAPTER 6
LETTERS FOR LITIGATORS

A. To Opposing Counsel – Requesting

1. Discovery Letter – Discovery Requests

Date

Name
Company Name
Address 1
Address 2
City, State, Zip Code

Re:

Dear _____:

Please find enclosed Plaintiff's Responses to Defendant's First Request for Production of Documents, together with Certificate Regarding Discovery that was filed with the court this date.

Sincerely,

Law Firm

Lawyer Name

Enclosures
cc: Client

2. Discovery Letter – Service on Counsel

Chapter 6 — Written Discovery Letters

Date

Name
Company Name
Address 1
Address 2
City, State, Zip Code

Re:

Dear _____:

Pursuant to your request, enclosed are copies of the Complaint and Demand for Jury Trial with Exhibits, together with Plaintiff's First Request for Production of Documents, that were personally served on your client on [Date].

It has been over six weeks since your client was served with this discovery and the responses are now overdue. Please let me know at your earliest convenience when you will be providing the responses.

Sincerely,

Law Firm

Lawyer Name

Enclosure

3. Discovery Letter – Overdue (Perfunctory)

Date

Name
Company Name
Address 1
Address 2
City, State, Zip Code

Re:

Dear _____:

Plaintiff served both defendants in this case with interrogatories and we also served [defendant #2] with a request for production. The answers to this entire discovery are now overdue.

Please let me know when I can expect to receive your answers.

Sincerely,

Law Firm

Lawyer Name

4. Discovery Letters – Overdue (Detailed)

CHAPTER 6

Written Discovery Letters

Date

Name
Company Name
Address 1
Address 2
City, State, Zip Code

Re:

Dear _____:

Pursuant to Massachusetts Superior Court Rule 9C, please consider this letter a discovery conference.

On [Date], I served you with interrogatories and requests for the production of documents on behalf of my client, [Name]. I advised you that your responses to requests for production of documents were due by [Date] and your answers to interrogatories were due by [Date].

To date I have received no responses from you to our discovery requests. This is notice pursuant to Rule 3-431 (h) that I will be seeking a default judgment unless you serve complete answers on or before [Date]. Please call me to discuss this matter *upon receipt of this letter.*

Sincerely,

Law Firm

Lawyer Name

5. Discovery Letter – Incomplete

Date

Name
Company Name
Address 1
Address 2
City, State, Zip Code

Re:

Dear _____:

This letter is prompted primarily by my review of the copies of documents you recently provided to us. Following my initial inspection of documents in late [Month], I sent you a letter, dated [Date], requesting copies of particular documents. My letter specifically requested copies of particular documents as a "first phase" of document inspection; it did not indicate that the letter represented all the documents being requested. None of the documents requested in my letter were produced at that time, and it took over four months for you to provide me with any documents at all.

As the attached chart reflects, you have still not produced many of the requested documents on even the more narrowly drawn list. More significantly, you have withheld many of the most relevant financial documents regarding the real estate entities, as well as _____'s personal finances and business expenses. The column farthest to the right on the chart shows what was produced. Clearly, there is much missing.

Furthermore, although you were served with Requests for Admissions and Interrogatories on [Date], you have neither served responses nor sought an extension from me for such responses. I would like to know what your position is on these discovery requests.

As you know, it is my philosophy (and the rules require) that we should resolve discovery disputes by ourselves when at all possible. Our ongoing cordial relationship certainly warrants such an approach. However, your lack of responsiveness on my discovery requests will, if not promptly rectified, force me to seek the Court's assistance—seemingly an unnecessary and unfortunate way for us to get through this. However, as time continues to pass, you are leaving me with little choice. There is much more you need to produce before I can commence depositions, and I will not be hampered by your delay as the discovery deadline approaches.

Please contact me upon your receipt of this letter so we may discuss these matters.

>Sincerely,

>Law Firm

>Lawyer Name

CHAPTER 6

Written Discovery Letters

6. Discovery Letter – Incomplete/Refused – General

Date

Name
Company Name
Address 1
Address 2
City, State, Zip Code

Re:

Dear _____:

Please consider this a good faith attempt to resolve a discovery dispute pursuant to Rule 2-431.

I am in receipt of your client's answers to interrogatories. You have objected and refused to answer interrogatory 20, which is identified in my interrogatories as Standard General Interrogatory No. 3, a court-approved form interrogatory.

The form interrogatories were adopted by Order of the Court of Appeals effective July 1, 1996. Your objection is therefore specious. Please supplement your client's answer on or before [Date].

Sincerely,

Law Firm

Lawyer Name

7. Discovery letter – Incomplete/Refused – Specific

CHAPTER 6

Written Discovery Letters

Date

Name
Company Name
Address 1
Address 2
City, State, Zip Code

    Re:

Dear _____:

Please consider this a good faith attempt to resolve a discovery dispute pursuant to Rule 2-431.

In your response to plaintiff's request for production of documents, **Request No. 11**, you have refused to produce the recorded statement taken from Christopher Witness taken on October 4, 1996, and that of the defendant.

Even assuming that these statements are work product, which I do not believe they are, Maryland Rule 2-402(c) allows a party to obtain discovery of documents or other tangible things prepared in anticipation of litigation or for trial by or for another party or by or for that other party's representative (including an attorney, consultant, surety, indemnitor, insurer, or agent) when the party seeking discovery has substantial need for the materials in the preparation of the case and is unable without undue hardship to obtain the substantial equivalent of the materials by other means.

My office has contacted Mr. Witness, who has advised us that he has no recollection of what he said in his statement. We have no means to obtain your client's statement other than by asking you for it. Accordingly, we are unable to obtain the information in the statements by other means, and the statements should be produced

Request No. 2 seeks copies of all documents that were identified, or should have been identified, in your answers to interrogatories. Although you identified the statement of Christopher Witness in a letter purporting to supplement your answers, you did not produce the statement itself.

CHAPTER 6

LETTERS FOR LITIGATORS

With respect to your response to **Request No. 3**, please produce the records you have "received in response to Subpoenas issued in this case."

You have refused to produce documents in response to **Request No. 5**, which seeks all documents upon which you will rely in support of any claim that plaintiff was either partially or totally disabled prior to the occurrence complained of, and in response to **Request No. 7**, which seeks all documents referring or relating to injuries, or treatment therefor, sustained by anyone in the occurrence complained of. You give no reason for your refusal to produce these documents, other than a conclusory allegation that the requests are "improper," which they are not.

Similarly, you have refused to produce documents in response to **Request No. 6**, which seeks all documents upon which you rely in support of your affirmative defenses. You give no facts to support your conclusion that the request is "overly broad, unduly burdensome and seeks to invade attorney work product." Discovery Guideline 5(c)(2)(ii) requires you to provide the following information in any objection based on work product: a) the type of document, b) the general subject matter of the document, c) the date of the document, and d) such other information as is sufficient to identify the document including the author and recipient. You have not provided this required information.

You have objected to **Request No. 9**, which seeks copies of all pleadings filed in any action involving prior or subsequent injuries sustained by plaintiff on the grounds that the records are "clearly obtainable by plaintiff," although you state you have no such documents in your possession. Rule 2-402(a) makes clear that "It is not ground for objection that the information sought is . . . otherwise obtainable by the party seeking discovery. . . ." Moreover, Discovery Guideline 5(b) provides that "The practice of objecting to an interrogatory . . . while simultaneously providing a partial or incomplete answer to the objectionable part is presumptively improper."

You have objected and refused to answer interrogatory **Number 21**, stating that the information requested is attorney work product. However, Maryland Discovery Guideline 9(c) requires you to provide the following information in any objection based on privilege (including work product): a) the type of document, b) the general subject matter of the document, c) the date of the document, and d) such other information as is sufficient to identify the document, including the author and recipient of the document and, where not apparent, the relationship of the author, addressee, custodian, and any other recipient to each other. You have failed to provide this information.

Please supplement your responses, withdraw your objections and/or produce the requested documents (or advise me of your refusal to do so) within the next five days.

                Sincerely,

                Law Firm

                Lawyer Name

cc: Client

CHAPTER 6

Written Discovery Letters

8. Discovery Letter – Follow-up to Document Request

Date

Name
Company Name
Address 1
Address 2
City, State, Zip Code

Re:

Dear _____:

My request for production number 7 requested production of all documents identified by you in answer to interrogatories. Request number 8 asked for all documents referring or relating to my client.

In your interrogatory answers, you referred to a surveillance video(s) taken by Commercial Index Bureau and photos of my client's vehicle, but you have not produced these materials. Please do so at your earliest opportunity.

If there is a cost associated with this, please send a bill and I will remit payment promptly.

Sincerely,

Law Firm

Lawyer Name

cc: Client

9. Discovery Letter – Follow-up to Interrogatory

CHAPTER 6

Written Discovery Letters

Date

Name
Company Name
Address 1
Address 2
City, State, Zip Code

Re:

Dear _____:

In your answers to Interrogatory No. 13, you refer to the following documents:

- Real Estate Appraisal by Al Keema & Associates;
- Contract of sale and related transaction documents regarding the sale of the property to Aames Capital Corporation;
- Contract of sale and related documents regarding the sale of the property to John and Amy Smith;
- Documents regarding the efforts of O'Connor Piper and Flynn to sell the property;
- Records of the Maryland Department of Assessments and Taxation;
- Records of the Carroll County Real Property Assessments;
- Carroll County Court records; and
- "Other public records."

I requested that you provide me with copies, at my expense, of all documents responsive to my request for production. The above-listed documents were not included in the copies you provided. Since Request for Production No. 6 requests copies of all documents pertaining to the plaintiffs or the property in question, these documents should have been produced. Please provide them now or advise why you are not producing them.

Sincerely,

Law Firm

Lawyer Name

cc: Client

CHAPTER 6
LETTERS FOR LITIGATORS

10. Discovery Letter – Supplement Request

Date

Name
Company Name
Address 1
Address 2
City, State, Zip Code

Re:

Dear _____:

Mr. White was examined yesterday at your request by your medical expert, Dr. Cohen. Please provide supplemental discovery responses, including a copy of Dr. Cohen's report as well as all the information required by Rule 2-402(e). I would also like to take Dr. Cohen's deposition and would appreciate it if you would provide me with available dates to facilitate scheduling at a mutually agreeable time.

Sincerely,

Law Firm

Lawyer Name

Enclosure
cc: Client (with enclosure)

11. Discovery Letter – Follow-up

CHAPTER 6

Written Discovery Letters

Date

Name
Company Name
Address 1
Address 2
City, State, Zip Code

Re:

Dear _____:

By letter dated [Date], I sent to you Defendant's First Request for Production of Documents and Defendant's First Set of Interrogatories. Pursuant to Rules ____ and ____, responses to those requests were done within [__] and [__] days, respectively. Both deadlines have now clearly passed, and no responses have been received. Please contact me immediately, and let me know when we can expect the responses. If we have not received full responses within two weeks, we will be forced to seek court intervention. Thank you for your time and attention.

Sincerely,

Law Firm

Lawyer Name

B. To Opposing Counsel – Responding

1. Discovery Letter – General Purpose

Date

Name
Company Name
Address 1
Address 2
City, State, Zip Code

Re:

Dear _____:

This is in response to your letter of [Date] asking about the status of my discovery responses. By now you should have received plaintiff's responses to your requests for production and interrogatories, which were mailed on [Date] and [Date], respectively.

With respect to your query about scheduling the plaintiff's deposition, I am not available in [Month] and would like to propose [Date] or [Date] as possible alternate dates. Prior to the deposition, and in fact within the next week if possible, I would like to have copies of the documents you indicated you would produce in response to my request for production, together with copies of records you subpoenaed from records custodians that I requested from you in my letter of July 3.

Sincerely,

Law Firm

Lawyer Name

cc: Client

2. Discovery Letter – Document Production

CHAPTER 6

Written Discovery Letters

Date

Name
Company Name
Address 1
Address 2
City, State, Zip Code

Re:

Dear _____:

Enclosed herewith please find Bates stamped documents 1-760, in response to your request for production of documents. These include medical records, bills, time cards and tax returns.

As I indicated at [Client Name] deposition, we are attempting to obtain an updated Subro Audit printout that will bring her medical bills itemization current, and we will supply that upon receipt.

Also as I indicated at the deposition, [Client Name] is still receiving treatment for her injuries, and we will supplement our discovery responses accordingly.

If this will not suffice in lieu of formal supplementation, please advise at once in writing.

Sincerely,

Law Firm

Lawyer Name

Enclosures
cc: Client

CHAPTER 6

LETTERS FOR LITIGATORS

3. Discovery Letter – Document Production Supplement

Date

Name
Company Name
Address 1
Address 2
City, State, Zip Code

Re:

Dear _____:

Enclosed herewith please find Bates-stamped documents 578-650 in supplementation to our response to your request for production of documents consisting of the following medical bills.

1. Dr. Michael Smith 2/98 to present $ 3,892.51

2. Dr. Marc Long 4/99 to present $18,469.00
 (Center for Pain Management)

3. Spine and Sports 2/98 to present $ 6,687.00

4. Mandy & O'Malley 7/97 to 12/97 $ 5,172.00

5. Dr. R.M. Kind 11/97 to 1/98 $ 2,974.00
 (Kind Chiropractor)

6. Hanover Hospital 11/17/97 $ 576.50

7. Hanover Diagnostic 11/17/97 $ 172.00
 Imaging

8. American Radiology 8/97 to 3/00 $ 3,673.00

9. Advanced Radiology 6/98 to 4/99 $ 26.00

10. Dr. Robert Brumbaugh 3/00 to 4/00 $ 311.00
 (Lower Chesapeake Orthopedics)

11. Union Memorial Hospital 3/98 to 3/00 $ 858.00

CHAPTER 6

Written Discovery Letters

12. Dr. Frank Johnson 12/98 to 1/99 $ 1,418.00
    (Mid-Atlantic Pain Institute)

13. GBMC 8/97 to 2/01 $ 945.35

14. Roundwood Imaging 5/8/00 $ 1,751.00

15. Children's Hospital 4/99 to 5/99 $ 1,029.62

16. Prescriptions 7/97 to 6/00 $ 252.08
    (CVS) & (Revco)

(Highlighted Items Only)

Subtotal: $49,733.06

Also enclosed are bills for out-of-pocket expenses incurred by Ms. White as a direct and proximate result of the occurrence totaling $1,369.61, for a total of $51,102.49 in economic losses (not including lost wages).

If this will not suffice in lieu of formal supplementation, please advise at once in writing.

        Sincerely,

        Law Firm

        Lawyer Name

Enclosures
cc: Client

4. Discovery Letter – Responses

Date

Name
Company Name
Address 1
Address 2
City, State, Zip Code

Re:

Dear _____:

With regard to the above-entitled matter, enclosed please find the following:

1. *Plaintiff's response to Defendant [Name]'s First Set of Interrogatories;* and
2. *Plaintiff's response to Defendant [Name]'s First Request for Production of Documents.*

Thank you for your attention to this matter. If you have any questions, please call.

Sincerely,

Law Firm

Lawyer Name

Enclosures
cc: Client

5. Discovery Letter – Interrogatory Supplement

CHAPTER 6

Written Discovery Letters

Date

Name
Company Name
Address 1
Address 2
City, State, Zip Code

Re:

Dear _____:

The following information supplements Plaintiff's interrogatory answers. Please advise me in writing at once if you will not accept this letter in lieu of formal supplementation.

Ms. [Client Name]'s employment information should be corrected to reflect her dates of service as follows:

> 1989-September 1991 (approximately): Clothes Boutique and Gem Vendors Company (both in Port Discovery, MD).

> September 1991 to present: Free Lance Graphics, Baltimore, MD.

Plaintiff may call the following to testify as expert witnesses, and one or more of them may also testify as fact witnesses.

Dr. [Name] and/or any health care provider who has examined or treated the plaintiff may be called to testify about plaintiff's physical injuries; her past, present and future damages caused as a result of the occurrence complained of; the past, present and future treatment required; and its cost.

Dr. [Name], c. v. attached, may be called to testify regarding the nature and amount of plaintiff's past, present and future economic losses sustained as a result of the occurrence complained of.

The police officer who investigated the occurrence complained of and who prepared the police report, Officer Smith, Central District, may also be called as an expert to testify regarding the facts as well as the cause of the occurrence and the resulting damage.

Plaintiff also reserves the right to call as an expert any expert identified by any other party to this action.

CHAPTER 6

LETTERS FOR LITIGATORS

In response to your request to schedule a deposition date, please be advised that I will check with Ms. [Client Name] and get back in touch with you with some available dates.

In addition, I will be providing you with copies of the documents referenced in plaintiff's response to defendant's request for production within the next two weeks.

Finally, please allow this to confirm that Jane of your office advised me today that the records deposition for [Corporate Witness Name] will not take place on Monday and that you will re-subpoena the documents.

         Sincerely,

         Law Firm

         Lawyer Name

Enclosure
Bcc: client

6. Discovery Letter – Expert Witness Disclosure

Written Discovery Letters

Date

Name
Company Name
Address 1
Address 2
City, State, Zip Code

    Re:

Dear _____:

Please allow this to supplement plaintiff's expert disclosure. Plaintiff may call as an expert and/or fact witness any and all health care providers who saw or treated the plaintiff, including but not limited to:

1. [Name of Liability Expert], [Address];
2. [Name of Treating Physician #1], [Address];
3. [Name of Treating Physician #2], [Address].

Plaintiff may also call as an expert any and all experts identified in discovery by defendant. Dr. [Name]'s c.v. has been previously produced; the c.v.'s of the remaining health care providers will be provided.

Dr. [Name] specializes in rehabilitation medicine and musculoskeletal disorders. She is expected to testify consistent with her reports and findings set forth in her medical records, including but not limited to the opinion that the forces transmitted during the collision of May 9, 2002, were severe and sufficient enough to dramatically increase [Client Name]'s facet arthritis and foraminal stenosis and caused permanent injury to the surrounding bones, joints, ligaments, ligamentum flavum, annular fibers and joint capsules. Dr. [Name] is also expected to testify that plaintiff's condition is permanent and will worsen and that plaintiff will require surgery as well as ongoing treatment, including but not limited to physical therapy, injections, and pharmaceuticals.

Dr. [Name] is expected to testify consistent with his medical records and deposition transcript previously produced, including but not limited to the opinion that [Client Name]'s back problems worsened after the May 9, 2002 collision.

The other health care providers are expected to testify consistent with their medical records.

This disclosure is in no way meant to restrict the experts' testimony regarding their treatment of plaintiff, or their diagnoses of plaintiff's past, present and future pain, injuries and losses caused by this incident. These experts are also expected to testify that the medical treatment they rendered was reasonably necessary and that their charges and those of providers whose services and/or medications they prescribed or recommended were fair and reasonable.

If this will not suffice in lieu of formal supplementation to plaintiff's responses to discovery, please advise at once in writing.

                        Sincerely,

                        Law Firm

                        Lawyer Name

Enclosure

7. Discovery Letter – Follow-up – Continuance

CHAPTER 6

Written Discovery Letters

Date

Name
Company Name
Address 1
Address 2
City, State, Zip Code

Re:

Dear _____:

I am writing to confirm our telephone conversation yesterday in which you gave me an additional 30 days in which to respond to your discovery requests. By my calculations, the responses will now be due on July 20.

Thank you very much for your courtesy.

        Sincerely,

        Law Firm

        Lawyer Name

Enclosures

cc: Client

C. To Client

1. Discovery Letter – Client – Request Interrogatory Response

Date

Name
Company Name
Address 1
Address 2
City, State, Zip Code

    Re:

Dear _____:

Please be advised that the plaintiff in the above-entitled action has served a set of interrogatories, or written questions, which you must answer. Interrogatories are a common method of discovery in litigation used by one side to learn information from the other. You must respond to them fully and accurately, and then sign them under oath.

I would be grateful if you would prepare draft answers to the interrogatories and return these to my attention on or before [Date]. We will then prepare final answers based upon the information you have provided us and the information in the file, and return them to you for your signature.

[I have enclosed for your reference a general instruction form regarding interrogatories. You should read this form before preparing your answers.]

Should you have any questions, or if there is anything I can do to facilitate the process for you, please let me know. Thank you for your attention and cooperation in this matter.

                                  Sincerely,

                                  Law Firm

                                  Lawyer Name

2. Discovery Letter – Client – Requesting Document Response

CHAPTER 6

Written Discovery Letters

Date

Name
Company Name
Address 1
Address 2
City, State, Zip Code

    Re:

Dear _____:

The attorney representing the plaintiff in your case has submitted a formal written request that you produce documents for inspection and copying. This is a common method of discovery in litigation. The document request is enclosed with this letter.

On a separate sheet of paper, respond to each request to the best of your ability, numbering your responses to correspond with the requests, and indicating what requested documents you have or can obtain. You are required to produce all requested documents that are in your possession or control, unless I determine that a particular document (or documents) is privileged, wholly irrelevant, or otherwise objectionable. Attach all requested documents to your responses. If no documents for a particular request exist, simply state this in your response. It is very important that your answers are complete, accurate and truthful.

If at all possible, please return your responses to me within ten days from the date of this letter. Keep the enclosed request for your files together with a copy of your written responses.

When I receive your written responses and the documents themselves, I will have the responses typed in final form, and I will then contact you to go over them with you.

                Sincerely,

                Law Firm

                Lawyer Name

Enclosure

3. Discovery Letter – Client – Forward Draft Interrogatory Response

Date

Name
Company Name
Address 1
Address 2
City, State, Zip Code

    Re:

Dear _____:

Enclosed is "Plaintiff's Response to Defendant's Interrogatories" for your review and signature. Remember that your signature is under oath, so it is very important that you take the time to make sure that your answers are accurate and complete. If the answers are correct, **please sign page 12** where indicated. If you find any errors, please make the necessary corrections and call me so I can incorporate them and send you a revised document for signature. Time is of the essence; we would like to serve this response on the defendant no later than **Tuesday of next week**.

Please contact me if you have any questions or comments. Thank you in advance for your promptness in this matter.

                        Sincerely,

                        Law Firm

                        Lawyer Name

Enclosures

4. Discovery Letter – Client – Interrogatory Response

Date

Name
Company Name
Address 1
Address 2
City, State, Zip Code

Re:

Dear _____:

We have been served with interrogatories, a copy of which is attached. This letter explains what they are and how to answer them.

1. WHAT ARE INTERROGATORIES? The other side has served us with Interrogatories, which are simply written questions, which generally must be answered. *You must return your draft answers to us within 10 days, written on a separate sheet of paper.* You are required to answer these under the Massachusetts Rules of Civil Procedure.

2. PROCEDURE - After we have received your draft answers, we will review them, add information we know and then have you sign the final copy under oath. It is very important that these be complete and accurate. Your credibility is at stake. Moreover, you must not leave out any witnesses or information, because to do so will eventually hurt your case. For example, the penalty for leaving out any witness is that that witness may be barred from testifying at your trial.

3. POST-OCCURRENCE WITNESSES - Post-occurrence witnesses mean all people who saw you after the accident who might be able to testify to how your condition was before the accident as well as after the accident. These persons would include your employer, friends and neighbors who could tell about your condition and also your employment. Other types of witnesses would include persons who were at the scene right after the accident although possibly not witnesses to the actual accident.

4. DOCTOR VISITS AND BILLS - If you do not know the dates that you have gone to your doctor, you should call and ask his office secretary to send you a bill indicating these dates, or have her give you these dates over the phone. We will need to know the current bills to date for the total amount of services growing out of charges for this accident. Be sure it is the *total* amount and *for this occurrence only*. When we request bills, we mean all the bills from all hospitals, doctors, druggists, physical therapists, etc. Do not leave any of these out of your answers.

CHAPTER 6

LETTERS FOR LITIGATORS

5. OTHER ACCIDENTS OR INJURIES - When we ask you about prior accidents (accidents or injuries before this one), be sure that you indicate the date the doctor treated you, the nature of the accident and the nature of your injuries. It is very important that you indicate all previous accidents and all previous injuries. This means such injuries as childhood falls, football injuries, war injuries and the like. If you have had a previous back or neck injury, for example, there is nothing wrong with this fact, as you may be more susceptible or more easily injured in a second accident. However, the failure to tell this could easily give the impression that you were trying to hide evidence or lie. *You must always tell the truth.*

6. SPECIAL DAMAGES - The phrase "special damages" simply means all your expenses. When asked to list all special damages or all losses, list all of your expenses from the accident, including such things as the following: (1) doctor bills; (2) hospital bills; (3) car repair bills; (4) physical therapy bills; (5) clothing loss; (6) costs of trips to the doctor and hospital; (7) wage or earnings loss; (8) nursing expenses; (9) car rental; (10) housekeeping expenses; (11) brace, collar, wheelchair, crutches, etc., expenses; (12) baby-sitting expenses; and (13) drugs and medicine expenses.

7. ANSWER ALL QUESTIONS IF POSSIBLE - There are some questions on the interrogatories, for example, concerning whether or not photographs have been taken of the vehicles, which only we would know about. We will answer these questions when we receive your answers. If you, however, know about photographs, or know anything about any of the questions, you should so answer on a separate sheet of paper.

8. QUESTIONS AND HELP IN ANSWERING - If you have any questions, please do not hesitate to contact us. However, it will save us time if you take more care and more detail in preparing your own answers. This will also help you later when you have to give your deposition under oath. Keep a copy of your answers for your future reference.

Sincerely,

Law Firm

Lawyer Name

Enclosures

5. Discovery Letter – Client – Discovery Meeting

CHAPTER 6

Written Discovery Letters

Date

Name
Company Name
Address 1
Address 2
City, State, Zip Code

Re:

Dear _____:

Enclosed herewith please find four sets of "interrogatories" or questions that you will need to answer under oath in writing.

Please read these questions carefully and think about your answers before our meeting on [Date], at [Time].

Also enclosed are amended notices of deposition duces tecum for your depositions, now rescheduled for [Date], Ann at [Time] and David at [Time]. Please collect the records requested to the extent that I don't already have them. You must bring them to our meeting on [Date].

At that meeting, in addition to getting ready for your depositions, we will go over these questions and discuss how they should be answered. After our meeting, I will place your answers in final form and will then forward them to you for signature.

Please do not hesitate to contact me in the interim if you have any questions.

Sincerely,

Law Firm

Lawyer Name

Enclosures

6. Discovery Letter – Client – Responses

Date

Name
Company Name
Address 1
Address 2
City, State, Zip Code

Re:

Dear _____:

I have not yet received the information I requested in my letter of [Date], which I need to answer the interrogatories (questions) the other side sent us. **If we do not respond on time, this can hurt your case.**

Please call my office as soon as possible to set up a meeting next week so we can finish these responses. Please bring all the documents that were requested to our meeting next week. Even if you are unable to get all the information and documents together, we will still need to meet so we can figure out what questions we _can_ answer.

If illness or some other problem is preventing you from working on these requests, please let me know so I can take the necessary steps with the opposing counsel and/or the court to try to obtain another extension of time.

I look forward to hearing from you within the next few days either to set up a meeting or to discuss any problems that may be preventing you from meeting with me or completing the responses. Thank you.

Sincerely,

Law Firm

Lawyer Name

7. Discovery Letter – Client – Requesting Documents

CHAPTER 6

Written Discovery Letters

Date

Name
Company Name
Address 1
Address 2
City, State, Zip Code

Re:

Dear _____:

As counsel for [Medical Group [Business Name]], I recently visited your office to discuss the [Case Name] matter with [Managing Physician]. Dr. [Managing Physician] advised me to contact you to obtain the various documents we will need as we respond to the plaintiffs' requests. In this regard, I would appreciate your providing me with the following documents:

1. Any written agreements between [Medical Group [Business Name]] and [Plaintiff or Co-Defendants] that were in effect in [Relevant Date Period];

2. A date when I may review (a) the corporate by-laws that were in effect in [Relevant Dates], (b) any rules and regulations that apply to the company personnel that were in effect in [Relevant Dates], and (c) any other documents that reveal the extent to which [Business Name] controlled Physician Names, Agents, Employees, etc.;

3. Articles of Organization of [Business Name];

4. Charter of [Business Name];

5. Tax records for [Business Name], fiscal years _____;

6. If [Business Name] is a non-profit organization, we will want to obtain any documents that will substantiate its charitable status; and

7. Employment contracts, W-2 forms, and other evidence of the employment of [Named Defendant Physicians, etc.].

Our request for documents (see item 6 above) is limited to records from the IRS or Department of Revenue that demonstrate in [Relevant Years] that

CHAPTER 6

LETTERS FOR LITIGATORS

these agencies considered [Business Name] a charity, such as a "letter of determination."

Our request for the by-laws and the written agreements between [Business Name] and the [Plaintiffs' Healthcare Providers] are part of our attempt to locate documents that demonstrate the extent to which [Business Name] had the right to control these physicians.

And finally, if there is anything we can do to limit the time and effort required to provide us with the requested information, please notify me. Your attention to these matters and your ongoing assistance is greatly appreciated. Thank you.

                                            Sincerely,

                                            Law Firm

                                            Lawyer Name

cc: Insurance company client

CHAPTER 7

Deposition/Examination

Depositions can be confusing for a client who is new to litigation. Use carefully crafted letters to take the mystery out of a deposition notice or subpoena duces tecum and give the process clarity. When scheduling multiple depositions, use letters to memorialize changes in date and time that may not appear in the original notices. Once depositions are complete, the letter transmitting the errata sheet serves as a diary reminder to have the client or witness complete his or her review of the transcript.

It's a good idea to check with opposing counsel before scheduling and noticing a deposition. If, for whatever reason, you failed to do this, send a letter along with the deposition notice offering to reschedule at a mutually agreeable time.

CHAPTER 7

LETTERS FOR LITIGATORS

A. To Opposing Counsel

1. Deposition Letter – Scheduling

Date

Name
Company Name
Address 1
Address 2
City, State, Zip Code

Re:

Dear _____:

Enclosed please find deposition notice duces tecum for Mr. [Opposing Party] on the date you selected. I understand you will not be making an issue about the 30-day notice requirement for documents, as this deposition was previously noticed and then postponed at your request and the requisite 30 days' notice has already been given.

I will also be noticing a corporate designee deposition of [Corporation] for later this same day and ask that you hold this time open on your calendar and alert your client, if he is the corporate designee, to do the same.

Finally, please provide me with the items requested in my Request for Production No. 5 that pertain to your experts, namely, curriculum vitae, reports, materials relied upon, and any correspondence with or documents generated by them (including their bills and any correspondence with you). As you know, these experts were not timely designated and I reserve the right to object to their testimony, particularly if there is any further delay in production of these documents, which were requested long ago.

Sincerely,

Law Firm

Lawyer Name

cc: Client

2. Deposition Letter – Scheduling (Alternate)

Deposition/
Examination

Date

Name
Company Name
Address 1
Address 2
City, State, Zip Code

    Re:

Dear _____:

This is in response to your letter of [Date] asking about the status of my discovery responses. By now you should have received plaintiff's responses to your requests for production and interrogatories, which were mailed on [Date] and [Date], respectively.

With respect to your query about scheduling the plaintiff's deposition, I am not available in [Month] and would like to propose [Date] or [Date] as possible alternate dates. Prior to the deposition, and in fact within the next week if possible, I would like to have copies of the documents you indicated you would produce in response to my request for production, together with copies of records you subpoenaed from records custodians that I requested from you in my letter of [Date].

                  Sincerely,

                  Law Firm

                  Lawyer Name

cc: Client

CHAPTER 7

LETTERS FOR LITIGATORS

3. Medical Examination – Scheduling

Date

Name
Company Name
Address 1
Address 2
City, State, Zip Code

    Re:

Dear _____:

This is to confirm our phone conversation of August 10.

With respect to your inquiry about Ms. [Client Name]'s availability for a defense medical exam, I advised that we will make her available after you have provided us with copies of the documents you indicated you would produce in response to my request for production, together with copies of the records you subpoenaed that I requested in my letters of [Date] and [Date].

We would prefer that the examination be scheduled on either a Tuesday or Wednesday to be completed no later than [Time]. When you have some possible dates, please let me know and I will check with my client to confirm her availability.

                      Sincerely,

                      Law Firm

                      Lawyer Name

Enclosures
cc: Client

B. To Client

1. Deposition Letter – Notice

CHAPTER 7
Deposition/
Examination

Date

Name
Company Name
Address 1
Address 2
City, State, Zip Code

    Re:

Dear _____:

Enclosed herewith please find notices of deposition rescheduling your depositions for [Date], Ann at [Time] and David at [Time]. We have agreed to meet in my office at [Time] on [Date] to prepare.

If you have any documents that are requested in these deposition notices that you have not already provided to me, please bring them to our meeting on [Date].

Please do not hesitate to contact me in the interim if you have any questions. I'm looking forward to seeing you on [Date].

                    Sincerely,

                      Law Firm

                      Lawyer Name

Enclosures

2. Deposition Letter – Scheduling Letter

Date

Name
Company Name
Address 1
Address 2
City, State, Zip Code

Re:

Dear _____:

As a follow-up to our telephone conversation of this morning, this letter is to confirm that you will attend and testify at your deposition on [Date] at [Time] at the law offices of [Firm Name and Location]. Enclosed are directions to the firm to assist you.

This is also to confirm our arrangement to meet at [Location], on [Date], at [Time] to prepare you for your deposition. Enclosed is a copy of our firm brochure, "A Deposition . . . what is that?" for your review. Should you have any questions, please call me.

Sincerely,

Law Firm

Lawyer Name

Enclosures

3. Deposition Letter – Review Transcript

CHAPTER 7

Deposition/
Examination

Date

Name
Company Name
Address 1
Address 2
City, State, Zip Code

Re:

Dear _____:

Enclosed please find a copy of the transcript from your deposition, which was taken on [Day][Date]. Please carefully review your testimony as transcribed by the court reporter. If you believe there are any errors in the transcription of your testimony, please make any changes you may have on the enclosed copy of the Errata Sheet. Also, if you believe any statements are not substantively correct, please contact me immediately so we may discuss this.

Once you have reviewed the transcript, please sign it on the signature page where I have indicated, and return the original transcript to me no later than [Date].

If you have any questions, please feel free to contact me.

Sincerely,

Law Firm

Lawyer Name

Enclosure

4. Deposition Letter – Errata Sheet

Date

Name
Company Name
Address 1
Address 2
City, State, Zip Code

Re:

Dear _____:

Enclosed please find the typed Errata Sheet for your deposition, based on your draft and our discussions. Please review it carefully with the transcript, sign it and return it to me. If you have any questions, please contact me to discuss it as soon as possible, as the time limit is approaching.

Also enclosed are recent pleadings and correspondence regarding your case. In a nutshell, the court granted our motion to prevent the examination by Dr. Black, but [Opposing Counsel] has requested a reconsideration of this ruling, and we have opposed it. We also won our motion to force [Opposing Counsel] to supplement his disclosure of Dr. Red's opinion, and a copy of Dr. Red's report is enclosed. We also defeated the defense's motion seeking to compel us to respond more fully to their written questions.

In addition, [Opposing Counsel] has hired an outfit called Commercial Index Bureau, which apparently took surveillance videos of you on [Date] and [Date] of this year. I have requested copies of the tapes so we can see them.

I hope you had an enjoyable Thanksgiving holiday and look forward to speaking with you soon.

Sincerely,

Law Firm

Lawyer Name

Enclosures

5. Deposition Letter - Status

CHAPTER 7

Deposition/ Examination

Date

Name
Company Name
Address 1
Address 2
City, State, Zip Code

Re:

Dear _____:

Please allow this to serve as a status report on your case.

The following depositions have been taken, or are scheduled to be taken, by [Day][Date].

Depositions taken:

    04/23/01 California Savings Bank
    07/09/01 Green Pasture Mortgage
    09/06/01 and 09/10/01 Northern Manhattan Mortgage (for records and to personally appear)
    09/07/01 Jerry Smith
    09/10/01 ABC Capital Corporation
    09/11/01 Charles Ramirez
    09/11/01 Michelle Ramirez
    09/24/01 Defendant Smith
    09/24/01 and 10/16/01 Democracy Credit Union (for records and to personally appear)
    09/24/01 County Funding
    09/26/01 Golden Gate Mortgage
    09/28/01 CCI Financial (for records)
    10/10/01 Mary Smith
    10/11/01 Jennifer Jordan
    10/11/01 Tax Preparers, Inc.
    10/15/01 William Smith
    10/16/01 Northern Trucking
    10/16/01 Rose Ross
    10/18/01 George Peabody
    10/18/01 Sarah Peabody
    10/18/01 Steve Peabody
    10/18/01 Malcolm Peabody
    10/18/01 Lucinda Peabody
    10/24/01 Garrett Peabody

10/25/01 Esme Peabody
10/25/01 Jim Peabody
10/29/01 Edsel Financial, Kim Grapeseed (personally appear)
10/30/01 Linda Saws, Knapp Smith
10/31/01 Jim Tomascello, Alpha Home Mortgage

As you know, we have a hearing on Wednesday at which I will argue that this case should be transferred back to Ventura City. There is no guarantee that this will happen, however. The court may or may not issue its decision the same day.

If the case is not transferred back to the city, our trial will proceed in Laid Back County, beginning on [Date]. The trial could take as long as [Time Period].

Once the court makes a decision on whether to transfer the case to the city, I expect that the other side will start thinking again about settlement and we may be asked to participate in another mediation session, which I recommend we do. In my opinion, the case will be worth less for settlement purposes if it is not transferred back to the city.

Finally, I enclose an accounting of the expenses incurred up until [Date] of this year on your case (not including my own in-house expenses for travel, long distance phone, postage, copying and the like). There are considerable expenses yet to be paid, for such items as deposition transcripts not yet received or billed, the mediator's bill, our expert witness's bill, and others. Accordingly, please send me an additional check for [$____] within the next several days to apply to these expenses. After you send me that payment and I receive all the bills from the court reporters for the deposition transcripts, I will be able to give you a good estimate of approximately how much more the expenses in this case will be.

As always, please call me if you have any questions.

                Sincerely,

                Law Firm

                Lawyer Name

Enclosure

CHAPTER 8

Motions

Because motions and orders are self-explanatory and are either filed with or emanate from the court, they are self-documenting. The only purpose letters serve with respect to motions, then, is to simplify and explain them. For example, when you are filing multiple motions in a non-e-filing jurisdiction, give the court clerk a concise letter itemizing the contents of your packet to serve as a docketing road map and as a double-check to make sure everything is indexed.

Clients can also benefit from a brief letter summarizing the contents of a motion or order that puts them in context. If possible, project a time frame for obtaining a ruling on the motion and offer your opinions on the potential outcome so the client can understand the motion's role in the overall proceedings. Likewise, when sending the client a copy of an order, explain the effect it will have on the litigation.

1. Motions – Pretrial Submission

Date

Clerk of Court at Courthouse
Address 1
Address 2
City, State, Zip Code

Re:

Dear Mr. or Ms. Clerk:

Enclosed herewith please find the original and one copy of Plaintiff's Pretrial Submission. The Pretrial Conference is scheduled for [Day and Date of Pretrial Conference] before [Name]. Therefore, we would appreciate your bringing these pleadings to the attention of the court as soon as possible

Please file the original and return a date-stamped copy to the undersigned.

Thank you for your attention to this matter.

Sincerely,

Law Firm

Lawyer Name

Enclosures
cc: [Opposing Counsel Name]

2. Motions – Multiple Pleadings

Date

Clerk of Court at Courthouse
Address 1
Address 2
City, State, Zip Code

Re:

Dear Mr. or Ms. Clerk:

With regard to the above-mentioned matter, please find enclosed for filing and the attention of the court the following documents:

1. Motion for Issuance of a Court Order Compelling Production of the Criminal Record of [Plaintiff Name];
2. Affidavit of Compliance with Superior Court Rule 9A; and
3. Defendants' List of Papers Filed Pursuant to Superior Court Rule 9A.

Thank you for your assistance.

Sincerely,

Law Firm

Lawyer Name

cc: [Opposing Counsel Name]

3. Motions – Court Order – To Client

Date

Name
Company Name
Address 1
Address 2
City, State, Zip Code

Re:

Dear _____:

Enclosed please find self-explanatory correspondence from me to our opposing counsel. Also enclosed are three recent court orders that:

- Dismiss [a third defendant] from the case (we consented to this because, since filing suit, we have learned that it did not assume any of the first defendant's liabilities in the buy-out; it therefore has no liability to you under Maryland law);

- Consolidate your case with the case brought by the other driver who was injured in this collision (we opposed this because we believe it will slow the progress of your case, but the judge probably feels it will save the court system time and resources); and

- Order that [defendants one and two] are liable to you for damages and prohibit them from disputing this at trial (meaning that the only issue will be how much in damages they are liable for). This is a very favorable ruling for you.

Please don't hesitate to call if you have any questions.

Sincerely,

Law Firm

Lawyer Name

Enclosures

4. Motions – Requesting Action

Date

Judge Name at Courthouse
Address 1
Address 2
City, State, Zip Code

Re:

Dear Judge _____:

As counsel for [Client Name] in the above civil matter, I am writing to ask the Court's assistance in moving this matter forward. This matter has been pending for some time, in part because Judge [Judge Name] dismissed the Complaint, and the [___] Circuit later overturned that dismissal. By the time the matter was reassigned to you, our client had run out of funds to pay counsel due to the Asset Freeze Order. On [Date], we filed with this Court a Motion to Modify Asset Freeze Order, to allow funds to be released to pay fees and costs. The ___ responded on [Date], but to this date there has been no decision from the Court.

We certainly understand the Court's busy calendar, but hope and believe that this is a relatively simple motion, which, if approved, will allow the case to go forward. We respectfully ask you to consider and act on this motion at the earliest possible date.

Thank you for your time and consideration.

                Sincerely,

                Law Firm

                Lawyer Name

cc: [Opposing Counsel]

CHAPTER 9

Trial

With trial approaching, the pace of litigation will pick up as multiple tasks will be ongoing simultaneously. Letters take on an increasingly significant role at this time in keeping the client, the trial team, and witnesses apprised of their respective roles and deadlines. While the temptation to make trial arrangements informally can be almost irresistible, the benefit to be gained from having everything documented cannot be overstated. Bear in mind that any letters you send to witnesses who are not your client are not protected by the attorney-client privilege. In most circumstances, it is advisable to limit the subject of written communications that could become trial exhibits to administrative matters such as scheduling.

CHAPTER 9

LETTERS FOR LITIGATORS

A. Client

1. Client – Scheduling

Date

Name
Company Name
Address 1
Address 2
City, State, Zip Code

Re:

Dear _____:

Please allow this to serve as a status report. The defendants filed an answer to our complaint; a copy is enclosed for your records.

I have also enclosed a pre-trial scheduling order regarding your case. Please mark your calendars; your attendance is mandatory at the pre-trial conference of [Date], and at the trial beginning on [Date].

Be aware, however, that the trial date is subject to change, and the trial itself may not start until a few days to weeks later depending on the condition of the court's trial calendar at that time. The trial may take as long as several days. It may be possible to settle the case before trial, but for planning purposes we must assume the case will go forward.

Please feel free to contact me if you have any questions or comments.

Sincerely,

Law Firm

Lawyer Name

Enclosures

B. Fact Witness

1. Fact Witness – Inquiry

Date

Name
Company Name
Address 1
Address 2
City, State, Zip Code

    Re:

Dear _____:

I am writing to you to follow up on my telephone message on behalf of [Client Name]. As an associate at the law firm of [Firm Name], I have been assisting [Client Name] with a potential lawsuit she may have against [Defendant Name].

[Client Name] believes that you may have witnessed an accident that [Client Name] was involved in on Interstate [__] on [Date]. I am hoping that you would be willing to share with me whatever information you may have concerning [Client Name]'s accident. If you could please call me at my office, I would appreciate it very much, as I would like to speak with you as soon as possible.

Thank you for your attention to this matter. I look forward to hearing from you.

                Sincerely,

                Law Firm

                Lawyer Name

cc: Client

C. Expert Witness

1. Expert Witness – Client Letter

Date

Name
Company Name
Address 1
Address 2
City, State, Zip Code

    Re:

Dear _____:

Please allow this to serve as a status report on your case.

I have met with our expert, [Expert Name], who has reviewed this matter in detail. He will testify on your behalf that [defendant] committed legal malpractice, which caused economic injury to you. A letter from [Expert Name] is enclosed for your records, together with a copy of his bill so far, which I have paid out of the funds you sent me.

I am enclosing a listing of the monies you have paid me and the monies I have spent on your case so far. You have a positive balance of $1,167.68. The remainder of funds were spent on [Expert Name] and the photocopies of [Defendant Name]'s file (the bill is attached; I have paid it). You will see from [Expert Name]'s letter that he expects to spend more time on this matter, and I will therefore be needing additional money from you in the future. Please bear this in mind for purposes of your financial planning.

I will continue to keep you informed of developments in your case, but please call me if you have any questions.

                              Sincerely,

                              Law Firm

                              Lawyer Name

Enclosures

2. Expert Witness – Deposition Review

Date

Name
Company Name
Address 1
Address 2
City, State, Zip Code

    Re:

Dear _____:

Per our recent discussion, please contact me within the next ten days to advise of your thoughts concerning the transcript of the deposition of our client, [Client Name]. Also enclosed are copies of transcripts of the other persons deposed in this case. Our deposition of the plaintiff is tentatively scheduled for [Date].

Also, pursuant to our discussion, we will be compensating you at your hourly rate of [$_____].

Your attention to this matter is very much appreciated. Thank you.

                  Sincerely,

                  Law Firm

                  Lawyer Name

Enclosures

3. Expert Witness – Medical Examination

Date

Name
Company Name
Address 1
Address 2
City, State, Zip Code

Re:

Dear _____:

I have made an appointment for you to examine and evaluate my client, [Client Name], who was seriously injured as a result of an industrial accident which occurred on [Date]. The appointment has been scheduled for [Day], [Date], at [Time]. By copy of this letter to [Client Name] I am requesting that he keep this appointment, and that he be prompt, cooperate fully, and, of course, be appropriately dressed.

FACTS OF THE ACCIDENT

On [Date], [Client Name], a 69-year-old deliveryman, was working for Office Auto Parts. A 100-lb. brake shoe fell and struck him on his right shoulder, causing a very bad injury.

TREATMENT

[Client Name] continued working for several weeks after the injury, but due to the pain in his shoulder, he had to stop working. Initially he sought treatment with [Doctor Name], a family doctor, and received cortisone injections into the shoulder as well as an MRI.

He was finally referred to [Doctor Name], an orthopedic surgeon, who evaluated him on [Date]. He was found by MRI to have a complete tear of the supraspinatous tendon with retraction. Surgery was performed on the shoulder on [Date] by [Doctor Name] at Blue Hospital. Surgery included arthrotomy of the right shoulder, Mumford distal clavicle excision, subacromial decompression and an unsuccessful attempt at repair of a massive rotator cuff tendon tear.

Following this surgery, [Client Name] had six months of physical therapy and regular follow-up visits with [Doctor Name]. He was sent for functional capacity evaluation on [Date], and it was found that he had specific functional limitations. Because of my client's desire to remain gainfully employed on a part-time basis, [Doctor Name] recommended vocational rehabilitation. A vocational assessment was in fact performed, and he is currently undergoing vocational rehabilitation.

PRIOR ILLNESS OR INJURY

Prior to this occurrence, in [Month], [Client Name] had a three-vessel coronary artery bypass surgery at Yellow Health Services by [Doctor Name]. This was a result of two myocardial infarctions complicated by congestive heart failure.

He has had repair of a right retinal detachment and macular hole in [Month, Year], and repair of a left retinal detachment and macular hole in [Month, Year]. He has had abdominal aortic aneurysm with endograft placements in [Month, Year].

For all intents and purposes, it appears that [Client Name], due to the shoulder injury, is permanently and totally disabled or, at least, suffers from a significant physical impairment/disability to the right shoulder.

I am attaching the following records for your review:

- Vocational Assessment, Small Vocational Services, [Date]

- Functional Capacity Evaluation, Union Rehab, [Date]

- Office notes, [Doctor Name], [Date] through [Date]

- Medical Records, Union Hospital, [Date] and [Date]

- Medical Records, AAA Repair, [Date], Yellow Health Services

- Records, eye surgeries and follow-up reports, [Doctor Name], [Date] through [Date]

- Hospital records, coronary artery bypass surgery, [Date]

I would appreciate your examining [Client Name] and providing me with an impairment rating as it relates to this gentleman's right shoulder.

                Sincerely,

                Law Firm

                Lawyer Name

Enclosures

cc: Client

4. Expert Witness – Scheduling

CHAPTER 9

Trial

Date

Name
Company Name
Address 1
Address 2
City, State, Zip Code

Re:

Dear _____:

Please call me at your earliest convenience to advise of your schedule (to the best of your knowledge) for July, August, September and October. Although the court has not set a date for the trial in this matter, we anticipate that notice of a trial date is imminent. If the trial date is incompatible with your schedule, I will need to notify the court and all parties to the conflict and request a new date. If you have any questions about the trial, please call me.

Thank you for your cooperation. I look forward to hearing from you.

Sincerely,

Law Firm

Lawyer Name

CHAPTER 10

Local Counsel

hen you are using local counsel or acting as local counsel for someone else, it's likely that the procedures and conventions with which you are familiar will be different from your co-counsel's. What's more, you and co-counsel will be working in tandem, but who does what may be unclear, because you may never have worked together before.

When lawyers from different jurisdictions work together on a case, letters are the perfect way to memorialize each one's responsibilities and to apprise each other of potential "local" issues. When lawyers share a client and/or a fee, it is critical to memorialize the work each lawyer is performing, and letters are one way to accomplish this.

Special ethical and professionalism concerns come into play when lawyers not in the same firm plan to share a fee. Be sure to check applicable statutes and guidelines before entering into fee sharing arrangements, and memorialize them in a letter so compliance is not in doubt.

A. Retention

1. Local Counsel – Fee Agreement

Date

Name
Company Name
Address 1
Address 2
City, State, Zip Code

Re:

Dear _____:

Thank you for calling today to discuss retaining me as local counsel in the above-referenced matter. As we discussed, Rule 1.5 of the Rules of Professional Conduct requires any contingent fee agreement to be in writing. It also prohibits lawyers not in the same office from sharing a fee <u>unless</u>

1) the division of fee is in proportion to the services performed by each lawyer, or, by <u>written agreement</u> with the client, each lawyer assumes joint responsibility for the representation;

2) the client is advised of and does not object to the participation of all the lawyers involved; and

3) the total fee is reasonable.

A copy of the rule is attached.

Accordingly, our fee must either be based on the proportion of services provided by each of us, or we must have a written agreement with the client that we assume joint representation. I interpret this to mean that if we want to divide the fee 50/50, we must each do equal work, or we must both be on the retainer agreement with Mr. [Client Name].

We will also need to memorialize the agreement between ourselves with respect to fees and expenses. I have prepared a draft which is enclosed for your signature or changes, as the case may be.

I look forward to working with you and Mr. [Client Name] on this matter.

CHAPTER 10

Local Counsel

Sincerely,

Law Firm

Lawyer Name

CHAPTER 10

LETTERS FOR LITIGATORS

B. Follow-up

1. Local Counsel Follow-up – Service

Date

Name
Company Name
Address 1
Address 2
City, State, Zip Code

Re:

Dear _____:

Service has been made on the defendant in the two cases we filed on behalf of [Client Name]. [Name of Prior Resident Agent] is no longer resident agent for defendant; our process server therefore had to make an extra trip, and his fee was $50.00 more than I had requested from you. I would appreciate it if you would reimburse me for the additional $50.00 fee (evidenced by copies of my checks payable to the process server attached hereto) at your earliest convenience.

Also enclosed are the affidavits of private process service that have been filed with the court.

Sincerely,

Law Firm

Lawyer Name

Enclosures

2. Local Counsel Follow-up – Experts

CHAPTER 10
Local Counsel

Date

Name
Company Name
Address 1
Address 2
City, State, Zip Code

Re:

Dear _____:

I have left several voice-mail messages with your office but have not heard from you. This is to advise that plaintiff's disclosure of experts is due on [Date], and that our answers to interrogatories are overdue.

It is essential that we designate our experts to the defendants in advance of the above due date. If we fail to meet our deadline, testimony from any physician, medical expert and/or health care provider, and any other experts, will most likely not be admissible.

I have enclosed a copy of the pre-trial scheduling order for your ease of reference, along with a form designation of experts from another case showing how designation of experts is accomplished in Maryland.

Please prepare the expert designation and forward it to me as soon as possible, together with Mr. [Client's Name]'s executed interrogatory answers. If there is a problem, please call me so we can take the necessary steps to obtain an extension of time.

Sincerely,

Law Firm

Lawyer Name

Enclosure

3. Local Counsel Follow-up – Discovery

Date

Name
Company Name
Address 1
Address 2
City, State, Zip Code

Re:

Dear _____:

This is just a reminder that I have not received the discovery that you want me to propound to the defendants. You stated in your letter of [Date] that you would e-mail it to me.

Since defendants will have 30 days to respond to the discovery and 15 days to respond to any motion to compel, you can see that we are running out of time to comply with the court order requiring all discovery to be completed, and all discovery disputes to be resolved, by [Date].

Sincerely,

Law Firm

Lawyer Name

4. Local Counsel Follow-up – Deposition

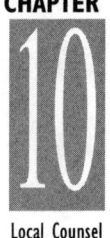

Date

Name
Company Name
Address 1
Address 2
City, State, Zip Code

    Re:

Dear _____:

This will confirm that Mr. [Name] 's deposition was completed on Monday. Pursuant to your instructions, I did not order a transcript. To obtain one, you can contact the court reporter, [Name of Court Reporter], Town Reporting Company, 100 Baltimore Avenue, Suite 201, Baltimore, MD 21204, 1-800-555-1212.

[Opposing Counsel Name] requested the name of the surgeon who performed [Client Name]'s bicep repair and [Doctor's Name]'s new address. As we discussed on the phone, he also requested that [Client Name] sign a sheaf of medical authorizations, which I told him you would be willing to authorize as long as he made certain stipulations and provided copies to you of all the documents obtained. I told him he would need to work the details out with you.

I also discussed the overdue interrogatories with [Opposing Counsel Name] and he stated he had not realized they were unanswered, but he checked his file and admitted they were, and stated he would answer them.

At this point, it seems that we should develop a demand figure and try to engage in preliminary settlement negotiations so we can determine whether the case can be settled or whether it will be necessary to start scheduling expert bene esse video depositions.

I look forward to discussing this with you further.

                  Sincerely,

                  Law Firm

                  Lawyer Name

5. Local Counsel Follow-up – Status

Date

Name
Company Name
Address 1
Address 2
City, State, Zip Code

Re:

Dear _____:

Please allow this to serve as a status report in the above-referenced matter.

The Court granted all five (5) of our requests for orders of default against the defendants. Counsel representing defendants [Names] contacted my offices on [Date], asking whether plaintiffs would consent to set aside the orders of default for those defendants. Please advise how you would like to proceed.

On [Date], we received interrogatories and request for production of documents from defendant [Name], responses to which will be due on or about [Date], allowing three (3) days for mail. Please provide the signed answers well in advance of this date.

Also, please send us on disk the discovery you want us to serve on defendants. Finally, we have placed several calls to your offices that have gone unreturned; would you rather we communicate via facsimile? Please let us know.

Sincerely,

Law Firm

Lawyer Name

CHAPTER 11

Settlement

Unlike most other aspects of litigation, it's not always possible or appropriate to document each and every step involved in settlement negotiations. It is imperative, however, to document the fact that you have conveyed any settlement offer(s) to your client and to document with the client your authority to make a particular demand or offer.

Once a matter is resolved with a settlement in principle, full-bore letter documentation should come into play to memorialize the client's understanding of, and agreement to, the terms of the settlement and the distribution of any proceeds. Having the client's written authorization for funds distribution will ensure that the client understands how much he will receive and will reduce the likelihood of a post-settlement dispute.

CHAPTER 11

LETTERS FOR LITIGATORS

A. To the Client

1. Settlement Letter – Demand

Date

Name
Company Name
Address 1
Address 2
City, State, Zip Code

Re:

Dear _____:

Enclosed please find a copy of [Plaintiff Name]'s formal settlement demand in this matter. Please realize that it is imperative that you treat this document as *highly confidential*; do not share it or discuss it with any co-workers, friends, or family members. It is particularly important that you do not share the demand with the co-defendants. Any disclosure could jeopardize a settlement. Once you have had an opportunity to review it, please call me to discuss your thoughts about it.

Also, please remember to return your deposition errata sheet and certification immediately in order to preserve your right to correct your testimony if necessary. Thank you for your attention to this matter.

Sincerely,

Law Firm

Lawyer Name

2. Settlement Letter – Offer

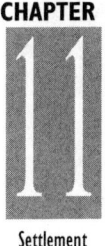

Date

Name
Company Name
Address 1
Address 2
City, State, Zip Code

 Re:

Dear _____:

The defendant's attorney phoned me this morning and offered $125,000 to settle this case. From our previous discussions, I know that you are not willing to settle for less than $250,000. However, as your counsel I am obligated to pass the offer along to you for consideration. The offer, while less than we would like, tells us that the defense believes that the case does have merit. I am therefore optimistic that we may be able to negotiate a better settlement than the one offered this morning.

As you know, the results in litigation cannot be predicted, and there is no guarantee that we will obtain a verdict larger than this offer at trial. Even if we do, there is no guarantee that the defendants would not appeal or that we would prevail on appeal.

Accordingly, please factor the risks involved into your decision about whether to accept or reject this offer. My recommendation is that we respond with a counter-demand to try to get a genuine negotiation going with the defendant.

Please give me a call to discuss this at your earliest convenience.

    Sincerely,

    Law Firm

    Lawyer Name

3. Settlement Letter – Begin Negotiations

Date

Name
Company Name
Address 1
Address 2
City, State, Zip Code

Re:

Dear _____:

As you know, we have just about completed discovery in this case, and the defendants know what our witnesses will testify to.

I would like to make a settlement demand to see whether there is any prospect of settling this matter before trial. As we have discussed, the results in litigation cannot be predicted. Even if we obtain a favorable verdict, the defendants may appeal, and even if we were to win on appeal, the mere fact of the appeal would delay your receipt of the funds.

A settlement would remove all of these risks and delays from the equation and bring this matter to closure. It would bring peace of mind and is therefore an option worth exploring. I have some ideas about making a demand that I would like to share with you.

Please give me a call at your convenience so we can discuss this.

Sincerely,

Law Firm

Lawyer Name

4. Settlement Letter – Finalize Distribution of Contingent Fees

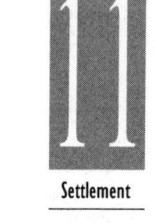

Date

Name
Company Name
Address 1
Address 2
City, State, Zip Code

    Re:

Dear _____:

Enclosed are the following documents that require your approval and signature:

(1) Release;
(2) Acknowledgments and Disbursements; and
(3) Authorization.

Please read all forms carefully. Kindly note that you need to have your signature witnessed on the release (1). The authorization (3) is not necessary, but makes it easier to forward your settlement check to you. If you choose not to sign it, you will have to come to the office to sign the check in person.

The release (1) and the Acknowledgments and Disbursements (2) must be returned to this office before you receive any settlement proceeds. The acknowledgment and disbursements explain how much money will be received and how the funds will be allocated. I have enclosed a stamped, self-addressed envelope for your convenience in replying.

I want to thank you for allowing me to represent you in this matter, and I look forward to receiving the above signed documents so that we can finalize the settlement.

Should you have any questions, please call me at your earliest opportunity.

                        Sincerely,

                        Law Firm

                        Lawyer Name

Enclosures

5. Settlement Letter – Closeout

Date

Name
Company Name
Address 1
Address 2
City, State, Zip Code

Re:

Dear _____:

Thank you for returning the signed settlement documents to my office so promptly. Pursuant to your authorization, I am enclosing my firm's escrow check in the amount of [$_____] representing your share of the settlement in the above-referenced matter. Also enclosed is an itemization of your medical bills that I paid out of the settlement proceeds pursuant to your authorization.

Please bear in mind that we have agreed to keep the fact of, and amount of, the settlement confidential. You should not reveal it to anyone; otherwise, the settlement could be jeopardized. If you have any questions about the settlement, or the confidentiality aspects of the settlement, please don't hesitate to call.

It has been my pleasure to work with you on this matter, and I am pleased that we were able to obtain a favorable settlement for you. Please feel free to call on me if I can be of further assistance on this or any other matter.

Sincerely,

Law Firm

Lawyer Name

Enclosure

A. To Counsel

1. Settlement Letter – Memorializing Settlement – Error in Release

CHAPTER 11

Settlement

Date

Name
Company Name
Address 1
Address 2
City, State, Zip Code

    Re:

Dear _____:

Enclosed herewith please find the signed stipulation of dismissal in the above-referenced matter in consideration for your payment of the settlement in the above-referenced matter, the check for which I have deposited in my escrow account.

The release you provided shows the other plaintiffs as signatories in addition to my client. This appears to be an error.

In addition, the last substantive paragraph of the release contains an indemnity agreement. This concerns me because the "payors" have presumably paid, or will be paying, monies to the other plaintiffs in this case to settle claims for alleged injuries that are arguably "traceable . . . no matter how remotely" to my client's claim. I do not believe it is your intent to have my client indemnify you for these sums, but in order that there be no misunderstanding, I would appreciate it if you would delete this indemnification provision.

Once these changes are made, I will have my client sign the release and will return it to you. In the meantime, I will continue to hold the settlement check in escrow.

It has been a pleasure working with you on this matter.

                      Sincerely,

                      Law Firm

                      Lawyer Name

Enclosure

2. Settlement Letter – Enclosing Executed Release

Date

Name
Company Name
Address 1
Address 2
City, State, Zip Code

Re:

Dear _____:

This is in follow-up to your letter of [Date]. Enclosed herewith please find the release you forwarded, fully executed by Ms. [Client Name].

The release is being provided to you in consideration of, and on the condition that you now forward the settlement check as described in your letter of September 19 so I can distribute the funds and dismiss the action.

Thank you very much for your kind cooperation in bringing this matter to a conclusion. It has been a pleasure working with you. Please don't hesitate to call if you have any questions.

Sincerely,

Law Firm

Lawyer Name

Ethical

CHAPTER 12

Ethical concerns can jeopardize the outcome of the litigation, the lawyers' involvement in the case, and quite possibly the lawyers' continuing ability to practice law, should a disciplinary body become involved. Discretion is always appropriate in this context, whether you are raising or responding to the particular ethical concern. While it is impossible to generalize about ethical issues, the importance of addressing them promptly and ethically, and memorializing the resolution in writing, cannot be overstated.

1. Ethical Letters – Challenge to Conflict

Date

Name
Company Name
Address 1
Address 2
City, State, Zip Code

Re:

Dear _____:

This letter will confirm our telephone conversation on [Date], regarding your firm's representation of plaintiff ALPHA Chemical Corporation in connection with the above-captioned matter.

As discussed in our telephone conversation, my client, OMEGA, Inc., has requested that your law firm, [Firm Name], withdraw from the representation of plaintiff ALPHA in connection with the above-captioned matter. As I mentioned to you, OMEGA retained your law firm in connection with a labor matter, which is ongoing and for which your firm has billed Omega over $100,000 as of this date.

Despite your representation of OMEGA in this labor matter, your firm is also acting as counsel for plaintiff ALPHA in its above-described action against OMEGA in the United States District Court for the Western District of Pennsylvania. We believe that this constitutes a conflict of interest for your law firm.

I am advised that your law firm did not disclose nor did it seek a waiver from OMEGA regarding your representation of ALPHA in the above-captioned action against OMEGA. I am further advised that Mr. Sam Smith, Esquire, whose name appears as counsel on behalf of ALPHA in the above-captioned case, also has performed legal work for OMEGA in connection with the labor matter. Thus, it appears that the conflict was known or certainly should have been known.

In writing this letter and stating our position regarding your firm's conflict of interest, I am relying upon my general understanding of ethics rules, particularly as they apply in the state of Maryland. I have not researched Pennsylvania law on this point, but I do believe that your firm would be required to obtain a waiver from OMEGA before representing plaintiff in the above-captioned action. Despite our strong belief that your representation of plaintiff in the above-captioned action creates a conflict of interest, if you are aware of any Pennsylvania authority to the contrary, I would certainly be willing to consider it.

I understand that you will advise me promptly regarding your firm's decision to voluntarily withdraw from representation of plaintiff in the above-captioned case. Although I am authorized to file a motion to disqualify, I am hopeful that your firm will agree to withdraw voluntarily.

                Sincerely,

                Law Firm

                Lawyer Name

cc: [Client Name]

2. Ethical Letters – Conflict – Individual

Date

Name
Company Name
Address 1
Address 2
City, State, Zip Code

Re:

Dear _____:

This law firm has been retained by the Big Institute, Inc. (BII) in connection with matters arising out of the Exclusive License Agreement, which is the subject of the above-captioned litigation.

It is my understanding that you formerly served as legal counsel to BII in various matters, including but not limited to drafting the above-referenced Exclusive License Agreement with Other Company, Inc.; that you simultaneously served as counsel to both BII and Other Company, Inc., for some period of time; and that you currently serve as counsel to Other Company, Inc.

I am writing to advise you of BII's position that your continued representation of Other Company, Inc., in any capacity, constitutes a conflict of interest and a breach of your fiduciary duties and other legal obligations to BII. As former counsel to BII, you are in possession of BII's confidential and proprietary information and trade secrets, as well as other information revealed to you under the attorney-client privilege. Accordingly, your current and continued representation of Other Company, Inc., which is a licensee of BII and an adverse party in the above litigation, constitutes a conflict of interest under the Cannons of Ethics and Disciplinary Rules of the Supreme Judicial Court governing attorney conduct in Massachusetts.

Moreover, pursuant to the same rules, your withdrawal as counsel is required because you are a potential witness, and possibly even a third-party defendant, in connection with the above litigation.

For the above reasons, BII demands that you immediately withdraw as counsel in any capacity whatsoever to Other Company, Inc. Please be advised that BII also expects you to abide by your ethical and legal obligations regarding the protection of BII's confidential and proprietary information, trade secrets, and other communications and information disclosed to you within the context of the attorney-client privilege.

If you have any questions, please do not hesitate to contact me.

Sincerely,

Law Firm

Lawyer Name

cc: [Client Name]

3. Ethical Letters – Contact with Employees

Date

Name
Company Name
Address 1
Address 2
City, State, Zip Code

Re:

Dear _____:

It has come to my attention that you have recently contacted several current employees of [Client Company Name], and have conducted telephone interviews with them, in connection with your investigation of the above matter. This was done without my knowledge or consent.

Your conduct in communicating with employees of my client without my consent is highly improper, and is in violation of Rule 4.2 of the Massachusetts Rules of Professional Conduct. See <u>Stanford v. President and Fellows of Harvard University</u>, M.C.A.D. Docket No. 97-BEM-4262 (1999); <u>Hurley v. Modern Continental Construction Company, Inc.</u>, No. 94-11373-RBC, 1999 WL 95723 (D. Mass. 1999). Moreover, I have been informed by at least one [Client Company Name] employee that someone from your office not only contacted him, but also made certain false representations to him regarding the status of the litigation.

While I have not yet determined what action, if any, I will take regarding your conduct, you are hereby advised to immediately cease and desist from any further contact or communication, directly or indirectly, with any employee of [Client Company Name] (or any parent or subsidiary thereof) without my prior knowledge and consent. Furthermore, I request that you provide me by [Date] with a written list of the names of all current [Client Company Name] employees with whom members of your firm, or anyone else on behalf of your firm or _____, have had any contact regarding this litigation (excluding the two depositions you have taken), including the dates of such contact, the method of such contact, and the substance of each and every communication you or your agents have had with all such employees.

Your failure to provide me with the above information by this Friday will leave me with no choice but to seek appropriate redress.

>Sincerely,
>
>Law Firm
>
>Lawyer Name

CHAPTER 12

Ethical

Administrative/ Other Proceedings

Administrative tribunals have special procedures that are as mysterious to the unfamiliar as litigation is to non-litigators. Letters, once again, come to the rescue and provide a way for the lawyer to put the process in context for the client. While most of the letters designed for litigation will also apply in the administrative context, we have included a few forms used in administrative tribunals that may also prove useful.

CHAPTER 13

LETTERS FOR LITIGATORS

1. Opposing Request for Postponement

Date

Name
Company Name
Address 1
Address 2
City, State, Zip Code

Re:

Dear _____:

I am writing on behalf of ABC Industries, Inc., appellant (ABC), in response to [Opposing Counsel]'s letter to you of [Date], requesting a postponement of the hearing scheduled in this case for [Day], [Date].

Although we sympathize with the situation of the chief procurement officer related in [Opposing Counsel Name]'s letter, it must be noted that ABC elected that this case be handled under the "accelerated" procedure provisions of the Board's rules. A postponement at this late date would disrupt the schedule for this matter as reflected in [Opposing Counsel]'s confirmatory letter of [Date], and the requirement under the Board's rules that a decision in this matter issue by [Date]. The position of the Maryland Transportation Authority that necessitated this appeal has created a substantial hardship for ABC in that ABC has only been paid about one quarter of the direct costs it incurred in performing its contract. This situation has contributed to a critical cash flow issue for ABC. For these reasons, ABC respectfully opposes the request for a postponement.

In the event that the hearing is postponed, we respectfully request that the duration of the postponement not exceed the three weeks requested by [Opposing Counsel Name], that if the postponement exceeds two weeks the date for filing post-hearing briefs be extended by one week, from [Date] to [Date], and that the [Date] date by which the Board is to issue its decision not be extended past [Date]. We also respectfully request that the Board's decision whether to grant the postponement be made by [Time] on [Day], [Date], and that counsel be given an opportunity to verify their availability and that of their witnesses in advance of the determination of any new hearing date.

Your attention to this matter is appreciated. Should you have any questions or comments, please contact me.

> Sincerely,
>
> Law Firm
>
> Lawyer Name

CHAPTER 13

Administrative/
Other
Proceedings

2. Enclosing Brief

Date

Name
Company Name
Address 1
Address 2
City, State, Zip Code

Re:

Dear _____:

I am enclosing an original and one copy of Appellant's Prehearing Brief for filing in the above-referenced matter.

The brief makes reference to several cases from outside of Maryland. If the Board members would like to have copies of the opinions in these cases, please advise and I will supply them. Copies of these cases have been previously provided to counsel for the Maryland Transportation Authority.

Your assistance in this matter is appreciated. Should you have any questions or comments, please contact me.

Sincerely,

Law Firm

Lawyer Name

CHAPTER 14

Government Investigations

Even though a government investigation is preliminary to litigation, it has equal, if not greater, importance. The letters an attorney writes in connection with a government investigation telegraph the perceived gravity of the matter as well as the extent to which the client will or will not cooperate. They can also rein in inappropriate conduct by the client and others under investigation. Your letters, if prepared ineptly, may spell the difference between indictment and exoneration. Now is the time for thoughtful reflection. Whatever time you spend wordsmithing in the context of a government investigation will be time well spent.

A. To Client

1. To Client – Confirming Letter

PERSONAL AND CONFIDENTIAL

                                                        Date

Name
Company Name
Address 1
Address 2
City, State, Zip Code

    Re:

Dear _____:

Just a short note to confirm our telephone conversation of [Day] in which you retained me to represent you regarding the [Government Agency] investigation relating to [Entity Name]. It was a pleasure talking with you, and I look forward to working with you on this matter.

I have sent the [Government Agency] a letter (copy attached) to inform them that I represent you, and I will let you know as soon as I hear from them on the logistics and timing of your appearance. Meanwhile, I am enclosing a standard retention letter for your review and signature, and a memorandum on testifying before the [Government Agency] that I have developed over the years.

I also wanted to confirm that we have agreed to meet in my office on [Date], from [Time Period]. Please bring your subpoena and any documents you think may be related to or useful in our preparation.

Finally, let me restate one very important piece of advice: now that you have counsel, do not talk to <u>anyone</u> about the case. Use me as the "bad guy" if necessary, and let me know immediately if anyone approaches you to discuss this matter.

If you have any questions on any of the above (or anything at any point in our working together), please don't hesitate to call.

>Sincerely,

>Law Firm

>Lawyer Name

CHAPTER 14

Government Investigations

CHAPTER 14
LETTERS FOR LITIGATORS

2. To Client – Joint Defense Cover Letter

Date

Name
Company Name
Address 1
Address 2
City, State, Zip Code

Re:

Dear _____:

I am writing to you in regard to our work in preparation for your testimony before the _____ regarding _____. As I have mentioned before, _____ has been cooperative in providing me with documents and information to help in preparing your testimony. In order to keep certain matters arguably privileged, we have entered into a "Joint Defense Agreement," which _____ now wishes to formalize. This is a very common and accepted practice, which allows (but does not <u>require</u>) cooperation between the parties. The enclosed agreement from _____ is a fairly standard and straightforward version of this. Please review it carefully, and if you have any questions, don't hesitate to let me know. Otherwise, if you could sign it and return it to me at your earliest convenience, I would greatly appreciate it.

Sincerely,

Law Firm

Lawyer Name

Enclosure

3. To Client – Scheduling Letter

CHAPTER 14

Government Investigations

Date

Name
Company Name
Address 1
Address 2
City, State, Zip Code

    Re:

Dear _____:

I am writing to follow up on our conversation earlier today to confirm the following scheduled dates:

<u>Practice Session</u>: [Day], [Date], at [Time], in my office.

<u>Interview with the Government</u>: [Day], [Date], at [Time], in my office.

<u>Grand Jury Appearance</u>: [Day], [Date], in the afternoon. We will meet in my office and walk over to the Federal Courthouse.

If you have any questions or problems with any of the above, please let me know. In the meantime, please carefully read (or reread) my memo on being a witness, and let me know your thoughts or questions. Many thanks.

                Sincerely,

                Law Firm

                Lawyer Name

4. To Client – Forwarding Transcripts

Date

Name
Company Name
Address 1
Address 2
City, State, Zip Code

Re:

Dear _____:

I am writing to follow up on our various conversations regarding the transcripts of your _____ testimony of _____ and _____. As we agreed, I am enclosing a copy of both transcripts. It is very important that you review them carefully (with the same precision that we tried to use in testifying) for typographical errors, mistakes, and any problems that come to mind. Please feel free to write any changes, notes, or comments directly on the transcripts, and return them to me as soon as possible. We will then put all the comments together and submit error sheets to the _____. I also wanted to confirm that you have agreed to share the transcripts with _____, the law firm representing _____.

As always, if you have any problems or questions, please don't hesitate to call. Many thanks.

Sincerely,

Law Firm

Lawyer Name

Enclosure

B. To Others

1. To Others – Letter to Agency

Government Investigations

Date

Name
Company Name
Address 1
Address 2
City, State, Zip Code

   Re:

Dear _____:

I have been retained by [Client Name] to represent [him/her] with regard to any matter before the [Government Agency] relating to [Entity Name]. My understanding is that the [Government Agency] wishes to obtain [Mr./Ms. Name]'s testimony. If this is correct, I would greatly appreciate it if you could provide me with the [Government Agency]'s Order of Investigation and any documents or correspondence relating to my client, and contact me at your earliest convenience so that we can discuss logistics and timing. I look forward to working with you to help my client's involvement in this investigation proceed as smoothly as possible.

Many thanks.

                  Sincerely,

                  Law Firm

                  Lawyer Name

cc: Client

2. To Others – Third-Party Documents

Date

Name
Company Name
Address 1
Address 2
City, State, Zip Code

Re:

Dear _____:

I represent the [Client Company Name] (ABC), for whom your company has provided services. ABC has received an investigative subpoena from the federal government seeking a wide variety of documents, including documents relating to your company. ABC intends to fully cooperate with this investigation.

Whether or not your company has already received a similar subpoena or some other form of inquiry from the government, it may be useful for all concerned for me to discuss this matter with your attorney, as he or she feels appropriate. Therefore, I ask that you have your attorney call me as soon as possible. If you do not yet have an attorney representing you in this investigation, you may wish to retain one. If you need recommendations for reputable attorneys with significant experience in this particular area of federal investigations, I would be happy to provide you with some suggestions.

Finally, I would ask you to provide me with any documents or information you may have regarding any work done by your company on the personal property of any ABC employee, or anything of value provided to any ABC employee. Your timely cooperation would be greatly appreciated. Thank you.

Sincerely,

Law Firm

Lawyer Name

3. To Others – Government Records Response

Government Investigations

Date

Name
Company Name
Address 1
Address 2
City, State, Zip Code

    Re:

Dear _____:

I am writing on behalf of my client, [Client Name], to let you know that [he/she] has searched his/her files in response to your records request, as modified by our correspondence. The only responsive documents he/she has in his/her possession were previously turned over to _____.
Therefore, he/she has nothing further to produce.

If you have any problems or questions, please let me know.

                    Sincerely,

                    Law Firm

                    Lawyer Name

cc: Client

Other Publications Available from the ABA General Practice Solo & Small Firm Section

Qty	Title	Product Code	Regular Price	Section Member Price	Total
_____	Letters for Litigators	5150291	$80.00	65.00	$_____
_____	Letters for Lawyers, 2nd Edition	5150290	$80.00	65.00	$_____
_____	Package Deal: Letters for Lawyers, 2nd Edition and Letters for Litigators	5150292P	$128.00	104.00	$_____
_____	Real Estate Closing Deskbook, 2nd Edition	5150289	$99.95	85.00	$_____
_____	Attorney and Law Firm Guide to the Business of Law, 2nd Edition	5150286	$119.95	99.95	$_____
_____	Commercial Real Estate Law Practice Manual with Forms	5150287	$179.95	149.95	$_____
_____	The Lawyer's Guide to Negotiation	5150285	$79.95	59.95	_____
_____	The Effective Estate Planning Practice	5150283	$109.95	89.95	$_____
_____	Understanding Elder Law	5150288	$119.95	99.95	$_____
_____	Advising the Qui Tam Whistleblower	5150282	$94.95	79.95	$_____
_____	The Lawyer's Business Valuation Handbook	5130106	$124.95	114.95	$_____
_____	The Complete Guide to Divorce Practice, 2nd Edition	5150273	$125.95	115.95	$_____
_____	Going to Trial, 2nd Edition	5150277	$99.95	89.95	$_____
_____	Preparing Witnesses	5150272	$69.95	59.95	$_____

Orders   *Shipping/Handling
$5.00 to $9.99 .... $3.95
$10.00 to $24.99 .... $5.95
$25.00 to $49.99 .... $9.95
$50.00 to $99.99 .... $12.95
$100.00 to $349.99 .... $17.95
$350.00 to $499.99 .... $24.95
$500.00 to $999.99 .... $29.95
$1,000+ $34.95

**Tax
DC residents add 5.75%
IL residents add 8.75%
MD residents add 5%

Subtotal $_____
*Shipping/Handling $_____
**Tax $_____
TOTAL $_____

PAYMENT
❏ Check enclosed (to the ABA)
❏ Visa ❏ MasterCard ❏ American Express

Name_____ Firm_____

Address_____ City/State/Zip_____

Account Number_____ Exp. Date_____

Signature_____

E-mail address_____ Phone Number_____

Mail: ABA Publication Orders, P.O. Box 10892, Chicago, Illinois 60610-0892
❖ Phone: (800) 285-2221 ❖ FAX: (312) 988-5568
E-Mail: orders@abanet.org ❖ Internet: www.ababooks.org